THA

We appreciate your business!
You've purchased the finest, most
up-to-date legal information available.

Sign up for updates now to keep your title current.
The law changes quickly. To serve you better,
we recommend you put your title on subscription
services. It's easy. Just call **1-800-344-5008**.

SPECIAL DISCOUNT: Provide OFFER CODE **633264**
when calling and lock in **reduced subscription pricing**.

A subscription entitles you to automatic updates,
which may consist of:
- Pocket parts
- Pamphlets
- Replacement or ancillary volumes
- Looseleaf pages
- New CD-ROMs

Thousands of titles on west.thomson.com
You will find a broad selection of law publications
at west.thomson.com. You can search for titles
by topic or key word, or by browsing.

IT'S EASY TO
STAY UP TO DATE!

- Call **1-800-344-5008**

- Ask to put your title on subscription services to automatically receive all update materials*

- To lock in **reduced subscription pricing,** provide OFFER CODE **633264**

* Updates may consist of pocket parts, pamphlets, replacement or ancillary volumes, looseleaf pages, or new CD-ROMs.

Service representatives at **1-800-344-5008** will give you details on what you can expect and answer any questions you might have.

For thousands of other titles, visit west.thomson.com

© 2010 Thomson Reuters L-361747/8-10

Praise for *Inside the Minds*

"This series provides a practical and focused discussion of the leading issues in law today." – John V. Biernacki, Partner, Jones Day

"*Inside the Minds* draws from the collective experience of the best professionals. The books are informative from an academic, and, more importantly, practical perspective. I highly recommend them." – Keith M. Aurzada, Partner, Bryan Cave LLP

"Aspatore's *Inside the Minds* series provides practical, cutting edge advice from those with insight into the real world challenges that confront businesses in the global economy." – Michael Bednarek, Partner, Shearman & Sterling LLP

"What to read when you want to be in the know—topical, current, practical, and useful information on areas of the law that everyone is talking about." – Erika L. Morabito, Partner, Patton Boggs LLP

"Some of the best insight around from sources in the know" – Donald R. Kirk, Shareholder, Fowler White Boggs PA

"The *Inside the Minds* series provides a unique window into the strategic thinking of key players in business and law." – John M. Sylvester, Partner, K&L Gates LLP

"Comprehensive analysis and strategies you won't find anywhere else." – Stephen C. Stapleton, Of Counsel, Dykema Gossett PLLC

"The *Inside the Minds* series is a real hands-on, practical resource for cutting edge issues." – Trey Monsour, Partner, Haynes and Boone LLP

"A tremendous resource, amalgamating commentary from leading professionals that is presented in a concise, easy to read format." – Alan H. Aronson, Shareholder, Akerman Senterfitt

"Unique and invaluable opportunity to gain insight into the minds of experienced professionals." – Jura C. Zibas, Partner, Lewis Brisbois Bisgaard & Smith LLP

"A refreshing collection of strategic insights, not dreary commonplaces, from some of the best of the profession." – Roger J. Magnuson, Partner, Dorsey & Whitney LLP

"Provides valuable insights by experienced practitioners into practical and theoretical developments in today's ever-changing legal world." – Elizabeth Gray, Partner, Willkie, Farr & Gallagher LLP

"This series provides invaluable insight into the practical experiences of lawyers in the trenches." – Thomas H. Christopher, Partner, Kilpatrick Stockton LLP

ASPATORE

www.Aspatore.com

Aspatore Books, a Thomson Reuters business, exclusively publishes C-Level executives (CEO, CFO, CTO, CMO, Partner) from the world's most respected companies and law firms. C-Level Business Intelligence™, as conceptualized and developed by Aspatore Books, provides professionals of all levels with proven business intelligence from industry insiders—direct and unfiltered insight from those who know it best—as opposed to third-party accounts offered by unknown authors and analysts. Aspatore Books is committed to publishing an innovative line of business and legal books, those which lay forth principles and offer insights that when employed, can have a direct financial impact on the reader's business objectives. In essence, Aspatore publishes critical tools for all business professionals.

Inside the Minds

The *Inside the Minds* series provides readers of all levels with proven legal and business intelligence from C-Level executives and lawyers (CEO, CFO, CTO, CMO, Partner) from the world's most respected companies and law firms. Each chapter is comparable to a white paper or essay and is a future-oriented look at where an industry, profession, or topic is heading and the most important issues for future success. Each author has been selected based upon their experience and C-Level standing within the professional community. *Inside the Minds* was conceived in order to give readers actual insights into the leading minds of top lawyers and business executives worldwide, presenting an unprecedented look at various industries and professions.

INSIDE THE MINDS

Strategies for Trusts and Estates in Florida

Leading Lawyers on Navigating the Unique Aspects of Florida Law, Avoiding Common Mistakes, and Developing Trust and Estate Plans to Meet Client Needs

2011 EDITION

ASPATORE

©2010 Thomson Reuters/Aspatore
All rights reserved. Printed in the United States of America.

Inside the Minds Project Manager, Caitlin Keiper; edited by Michaela Falls; proofread by Melanie Zimmerman

No part of this publication may be reproduced or distributed in any form or by any means, or stored in a database or retrieval system, except as permitted under Sections 107 or 108 of the U.S. Copyright Act, without prior written permission of the publisher. This book is printed on acid-free paper.

Material in this book is for educational purposes only. This book is sold with the understanding that neither any of the authors nor the publisher is engaged in rendering legal, accounting, investment, or any other professional service. Neither the publisher nor the authors assume any liability for any errors or omissions or for how this book or its contents are used or interpreted or for any consequences resulting directly or indirectly from the use of this book. For legal advice or any other, please consult your personal lawyer or the appropriate professional.

The views expressed by the individuals in this book (or the individuals on the cover) do not necessarily reflect the views shared by the companies they are employed by (or the companies mentioned in this book). The employment status and affiliations of authors with the companies referenced are subject to change.

Aspatore books may be purchased for educational, business, or sales promotional use. For information, please e-mail West.customer.service@thomson.com.

ISBN 978-0-314-27200-3

For corrections, updates, comments or any other inquiries please e-mail
TLR.AspatoreEditorial@thomson.com.

First Printing, 2010
10 9 8 7 6 5 4 3 2 1

Mat #41096906

CONTENTS

Elwood Hogan Jr.   7
Partner, **McFarland, Gould, Lyons, Sullivan & Hogan PA**
IMPORTANT NEW CONSIDERATIONS IN FLORIDA'S
TRUST AND ESTATE PLANNING PROCESS

Brad A. Galbraith   31
Partner, **Hahn Loeser & Parks LLP**
ADVISING CLIENTS ON CREATING AND UPDATING
AN EFFECTIVE TRUST AND ESTATE PLAN

Leslie J. Barnett and Sara A. Tolliver   43
Partners, **Barnett, Bolt, Kirkwood, Long & McBride**
UNDERSTANDING YOUR CLIENT'S ESTATE
PLANNING NEEDS: CREATING THE RIGHT
STRATEGIES

Helen S. Atter, *Partner* and   61
Matthew T. Harrod, *Attorney,* **Wood, Atter & Wolf PA**
A NEW OUTLOOK ON TRUST AND ESTATE
PLANNING STRATEGIES FOR FLORIDA CLIENTS

Brian V. McAvoy   71
Partner, **Harter Secrest & Emery LLP**
CREATING THE RIGHT ESTATE PLAN FOR YOUR
CLIENTS IN A GROWING PRACTICE AREA

Appendices   91

Important New Considerations in Florida's Trust and Estate Planning Process

Elwood Hogan Jr.
Partner
McFarland, Gould, Lyons, Sullivan & Hogan PA

Surely, the year 2010 will be reported in history as having been (if death occurred) the least expensive year to die, tax wise, since 1916—the year the federal estate tax was introduced to our nation. Taxing the wealthy at death began in the United States with the Stamp Act of 1797. Other similar taxes followed—coming and going—but it was the Revenue Act of 1916 that introduced what evolved into the modern day federal estate tax and now reported on the infamous 706 IRS tax return. The situation of 2010 was caused by a legal quirk—not fully caused by our tax laws, but by the quirky action, or inaction, of Congress. This is the first year in my legal practice that our federal government was so divided that action necessary to keep the federal tax program on balance became impossible. The United States was left with an expiration of the Economic Growth and Tax Relief Reconciliation Act of 2001 (EGTRRA), Pub. L. No. 107-16, 115 Stat. 38 (2001), which has provided for gradual increases in the tax exclusion or exemption amount, as well as decreases in the estate tax maximum tax rate. The stark result of the repeal of EGTRRA, as of December 31, 2009, is that for the year 2010 there is no estate tax and no generation-skipping trust, and additional tax factors left "dangling" for the coming months, leaving estate planners wringing their hands.

Marianne Kayan, a tax associate and young tax attorney at Buchanan Ingersoll and Rooney, in Washington, DC, who has early earned a reputation of tax accuracy, wrote in *U.S. News and World Report*:

> Since most estate plans were created without anticipating 2010's lack of estate tax, the heirs of clients who pass away in 2010 could discover some unintended consequences. It's possible, for example, that assets would not go to a surviving spouse, if the estate plan was phrased to give the maximum amount that can pass free of federal estate tax to another beneficiary, for example. In 2010 that would be all the money in the estate, and nothing would be left for the other heirs—including a spouse.

On May 27, 2010, Florida's Governor Charles Crist signed a new statute, FLA. STAT. § 733.1051 (2010), which addresses the potential problem in the estate plans of Floridians created by the repeal of the federal estate tax. The new Florida law, retroactive back to January 1, 2010, provides the heirs of

IMPORTANT NEW CONSIDERATIONS IN FLORIDA'S TRUST AND ESTATE...

those who died or who die in Florida in 2010, and have an estate plan that relies on federal estate tax laws to fund the A and B trust, or other types of shares or trusts, the option of going to court to ask for judicial modification of the estate plan of the deceased. The law does not apply to estates with a clear anticipation that there would be no federal estate tax in 2010.

It is noteworthy that the Florida law requires the heirs to seek court determination. This Florida law will automatically be repealed at the earlier of such time in 2010 as the federal estate tax is reinstated by Congress or January 1, 2011.

Every attorney, estate planner, and CPA that I have spoken with considers the 2010 tax picture "a real mess." Many of us in Florida believe that if our tax and trust planning for clients are skewed by the "mess," we are glad to have the Florida Disclaimer Statute, FLA. STAT. § 739 (2005), to assist in some astute postmortem planning.

How Do You Approach a Legal Issue?

Today, after fifty years as a member of the Florida Bar, my practice is limited to trusts and estates planning and administration. In my early practice, I experienced almost the entire legal landscape. In speaking with local students, I explained my practice as a broad range of clients from one who wadded up a parking ticket, throwing it in the face of an officer, to first-degree murder.

The criminal law was the first to be discarded, and for about twenty-five years, I thrived in the courtroom primarily in plaintiff representation.

As age demanded a slower pace and the economics of my practice allowed a narrowing of clients, I found my legal excitement in estate planning with an emphasis on trusts. As to excitement, I believe that every lawyer must maintain a degree of excitement about his work and the good he can perform for his clients.

As I aged, my client base changed with me. I consider myself fortunate in that many of my current clients are those who have stayed with me throughout the years, adding their family members as newer clients.

Seeking the client's objective is foremost. In considering whether to use a trust in an estate plan, we must keep in mind that there are often other options that will serve the client's needs. I like to have the client tell me in their own words what they want to do for their family and heirs following their death. It then becomes my responsibility to carefully evaluate the client's desires; available assets, now or proposed; and then make recommendations as to a plan. The thoughts of attorney and client must be in sync.

With clients having substantial assets and their estates likely to be subject to federal estate tax, I ask for permission to talk with the client's CPA.

This conference, or conferences as the need may dictate, should be summarized to be sure the following elements have been discussed and established as goals of the client:

- Client's intention that their property—some or all—will be held by a trustee in client's trust.
- Client's property precisely identified.
- Client's beneficiaries must be clearly identified. In some cases such as in a discretionary trust, the client must clearly identify a "class." A discretionary trust is generally a trust in which the trustee is granted absolute discretion in the distribution of income and/or principal to beneficiaries. In a discretionary trust, the beneficiary has no interest in the trust property until distribution is made. Beneficiaries may include unborn heirs, or the beneficiary could be a charitable entity.
- Trustee or Trustees: The client must be comfortable and have full faith in the character and ability of their trustee to administer their trust. A child or close family member can often well serve in that capacity with little difficulties. But if the structure of their assets is complicated and business expertise will be required, then the office of trustee will require serious consideration.

Family Status

The age of the client, where he is in his profession, and the size and age of his family are important factors to consider.

The young married couples are the clients with whom you can be immediately straightforward. With the federal estate tax exemption at $3.5 million, or even if it drops in 2011 to $1 million, most young married couples will choose to use the Florida Estate by the Entireties, a special form of joint tenancy ownership available only to a husband and wife under the common law. They then should give serious consideration to the appointment of a guardian for their minor children should disaster strike, and again, the size of the monetary estate becomes important for decisions of the funds to be controlled by the guardian or a trustee until the child or children reach at least the age of majority.

A thoughtful attorney, by learning as much as possible of the client's family, can serve the children in the drafting of a testamentary trust to a degree the children and possibly the client will never realize. One such matter would be to guide the drafting to stagger the trust principal payments over a number of years. I have never known an eighteen year old that was mature enough to receive a $250,000 bequest upon the parents' death. As age and assets go up, we begin to advise the client of the benefits of the utilization of the "equivalent bypass trust" and the "marital trust," commonly referred to as the A and B Trust.

During this era of our married clients with children, the life insurance agent finds an opportunity to sell his product, with the need arising for the attorney to draft an irrevocable life insurance trust. I stopped using the term "insurance" in this capacity years ago upon the advice of a former IRS agent who advised me that that word was a red flag to IRS auditors.

The drafting of an irrevocable trust can provide the attorney with a whole new experience with his client's immediate family, and often his extended family, with the use of "crummy powers."

Eyebrows are frequently raised with the use of the term "crummy." As we have experienced in many of our documents, its name comes from the successful litigant's name in the case. In this instance, D. Clifford Crummy earned a favorable ruling in D. *Clifford Crummy v. Comm'r of Internal Revenue*, 897 F.2d 83 (9th Cir. 1968). Mr. Crummy wished to gift an amount equal to the annual gift exclusion and not pay estate taxes on the gift accumulation. The problem Clifford Crummy faced was that the annual exclusion only

11

applied to gifts that his beneficiaries had a "present interest" in, as opposed to a "future interest." In other words, the trust instrument had to place in the beneficiary a right that would qualify the gift as a "present interest." The beneficiary of a "present interest," of course, has the right to take the gift as soon as given and use it for the beneficiary's personal use. The tax planning problem was how to restrict the beneficiary's right to possession without losing the gift tax exclusion. Through the Crummy case, which the Internal Revenue Service acquiesced in Rev. Rul. 73-405, 1973-2 C.B. 321, followed by other rulings which followed the Crummy decision, a method was accepted to be known as the "Crummy Trust."

Significant qualifying restrictions are required, to wit: prompt notice of the gift must be given to each beneficiary, who then has usually thirty days to withdraw the amount of each gift. The time given for withdrawal has ranged from four days (quickly determined to be too short) to forty-five days. The reasonable time period for withdrawal has been generally accepted as up to thirty days after the gift is made. Thereby, by classifying the gift as a "present interest," the gift tax is avoided. A word of warning— the IRS still is not happy with its acquiescence and appears to be looking at irrevocable trusts utilizing "crummy gifts" with a strong desire to attack.

I will never forget an early experience when I drafted an irrevocable trust requiring crummy powers for a grandfather with a local bank serving as the trustee. After sending the annual "crummy letters" the first year, I received a panicked call from the trust officer reporting he had received a letter from a grandson requesting his annual gift so he could buy a bicycle. A quick call to the grandfather who may have spoken with the grandson cleared that up. Had it not, future gifts may have been terminated. This incident points out the duty of the attorney as to one of several matters of education that is necessary with the client's family members.

Later in a client's life, if fortune has shown brightly on his financial efforts, nothing has given me more pleasure than drafting, funding, and placing into operation a grantor retained annuity trust (GRAT). This trust demands a "wealthy client" who can afford to make large financial gifts to his beneficiaries and has the desire to do so to save the payment of U.S. federal gift tax.

IMPORTANT NEW CONSIDERATIONS IN FLORIDA'S TRUST AND ESTATE...

Preparing a GRAT is a team project involving the attorney, the CPA, and the actuarial. A good team can produce an excellent satisfactory tax result for the client and one in which its satisfaction is enjoyed by the taxpayer's family as well.

The GRAT is a trust that has a specific stated term, usually (in my experience) two to three years. The client—the taxpayer—retains an annuity interest in the trust, established on rates provided by the Internal Revenue Service, referred to as the "7520 Rate"-Applicable Federal Rate, allowing the taxpayer to receive an annual payment from the trust for the said fixed number of years. Upon the term ending, the trust balance is distributed to the trust beneficiaries. However, if the taxpayer (grantor) does not live longer than the stated term, the trust principal balance falls into the probatable estate and is subject to federal estate taxes.

I cannot say I approve of an attempted GRAT when the client is not experiencing good health. GRATs and the related trust and documentations that are required are very time consuming and expert demanding, and are, therefore, rightfully expensive.

I recently represented a client suffering from Parkinson's disease. He fully understood the GRAT rules, as did his beneficiaries. A conscientious decision was made to proceed with the trust, and unfortunately, the client died short of the stated term.

On June 15, 2010, H.R. 5486, 111th Cong. (2010) was passed, and if approved by the Senate, which is anticipated, will extend the "life term" to at least ten years. With the new ten-year requirement, the probability that the taxpayer will die short of the term and thus subject the assets held by the GRAT to federal estate taxation and probate will increase. This will, of course, greatly reduce the desire to consider the use of a GRAT for many tax planners. The effective date of the new law will be for "transfers made after the date of the enactment of this Act."

Living Trust - As It Has Evolved in Florida

Our history teaches us that trust documents date back to the English feudal system, and today, the living trust, inter vivos trust, or revocable living trust, has been blended with the testamentary provisions of a will, and has taken on a very important position in estate planning. Living trusts in Florida became a "hot item" about thirty years ago and have continued to be so, being pushed by some in the insurance field or estate planners who insist, primarily to the elderly, that a living trust is a must document for proper estate planning. Unfortunately, in Florida, many are misled in seminars, with free lunches, to believe that a living trust can save inheritance, federal estate, gift, and income taxes. All of these points are stressed in the seminars, although Florida has no inheritance or income tax.

In truth, the grantors (customers of seminars), in most instances, fail to be properly directed to the estate tax planning elements establishing a clear understanding of all methods of minimizing the liability of the federal estate tax, including the unified estate tax credit, the unlimited marital deduction, and the charitable gift deductions, each having its place in reaching a decision as to the need for a living trust and, thereafter, the drafting of such instrument. As to saving taxes, we have to be blunt but clear that no income tax can be saved, but then if the trust principal is of a taxable size for federal estate taxes, the same tax benefits can be utilized here through the credit shelter trust and the marital trust (A & B trusts). The tax savings result not because of the living trust but by utilizing Internal Revenue Code provisions of the credit shelter trust and the marital trust.

Another problem with such seminars is that little, if any, effort is made to point to the fact, much less explain, that different taxable "years" may be involved, which provide for varied exemptions. It takes a skilled preparer to clarify these possible choices and the effect of each on the client's estate. Stemming from the preparation of living trusts by laypersons, the courts of Florida have made it clear that "the giving of legal advice concerning the application, preparation, advisability or quality of any legal instrument or forms in connection with intervivos or testamentary trusts by a lay person . . . constitutes the unlicensed practice of law." *In Re: Florida Bar Advisory Opinion - Unlicensed Practice of Law Non-Lawyer Preparation of Living Trusts*, 613 So. 2d 426 (Fla. 1992). Per the seminars, dark shadows are placed upon the Florida probate process, placing many in fear of great expense for their children following their death. This false perception oftentimes leads them into becoming grantors of living trusts that they really do not need. While it is true that Florida has, in the past year, doubled most of the probate fees, the highest fee today is approximately $400, and the process of the administration of small estates and summary administration in Florida is just not covered in these seminars. Few attendees of these seminars are aware or advised that attorney's fees charged in probate matters include not only the strict, careful administration of the estate, but also tax matters, including forms 1040, one or more 1041 forms, federal estate tax form 706—and, in many instances, the fees charged for these living trusts, which are immediate out-of-pocket expenses, after considering future earnings of this amount, exceed what the heirs of the deceased will experience in fees and costs for the estate services rendered. Sometimes clients are frightened into the entry of a living trust because of their desire to "avoid creditors." It does not appear that many seminars cover the fact that this is an untruth, and with the exception of a well-drafted spendthrift clause, as long as the trust is a revocable trust, the assets will be subject to the clients' creditors.

If our clients choose to use a living trust and the primary intent is to avoid probate, they need assistance in being certain that all assets that can be subject to probate are titled properly in the trustees of their living trust. If an asset is omitted or later acquired and not placed in the name of the trustee, probate will still be required.

Most Florida attorneys I have come in contact with disapprove of homestead real property being placed in a living trust. Although title companies in Florida have become much more lenient in the last several years in accepting trust-held homesteads, still there is the nagging fear of losing the cherished constitutional homestead protection, subjecting the homestead to creditor claims.

On the other hand, I urge clients to take advantage of placing "out-of-state" real property in a living trust to take advantage of the legal "fiction" of classifying such a personal property for title transfer purposes.

Prior to June 2009, there were a few reported cases in Florida where a spouse used a living trust to circumvent the elective share provisions, which could reach only probatable assets, and because living trust assets were not subject to probate, the surviving spouse could be "cut out" of inheriting from the deceased spouse. Effective July 1, 2009, FLA. STAT. §§ 732.2025, 732.2045, 732.2075, and 732.2135, were revised to effectively eliminate this kind of action.

As we conclude our conferences with our clients, we want our clients to have all of the factors of advantage and disadvantage of the estate planning device available to them, so that an informed decision can be made.

Regardless of any inferences that might be drawn from the above comments that a living trust is undesirable, we must keep in mind that Florida living trusts are a fundamental building block for most of the estates that we Florida attorneys plan. It is often through a living trust that we use exactly the same testamentary provisions for sheltered trusts, marital trusts, QTIP, etc. In Florida, we often have trust requests, or it comes in the form of the preparer's recommendation, when a client is in poor health or if a surviving spouse reaches a point where they just do not want the responsibility of asset investments and even the receipt of income and paying bills. Generally, it is the extent of the trust assets that dictate the use of a living trust. Many clients start with the position that they are unaware that many of their assets are not subject to probate and, also, should not be the subject of a living trust, such as life insurance, IRA (retirement plans), and/or entirety property. Generally, these assets pass directly to named beneficiaries and/or by operation of law to a surviving spouse.

In Florida, no administration is necessary when personal property is exempt under the provisions of FLA. STAT. § 732.402 (2009), and non-exempt personal property, the value of which does not exceed the sum of the amount of preferred funeral expenses and reasonable and necessary medical and hospital expenses of the last sixty days of the last illness.

Florida also enjoys a classification of summary administration, FLA. STAT. § 735.201 (2002). This action is available when the decedent's will does not direct formal administration, as required by FLA. STAT. § 733 (2010), and the value of the entire estate, subject to administration in Florida, is less than the value of property exempt, as stated above, and does not exceed in value the sum of $75,000. Sometimes a procedure that is overlooked occurs when the decedent's only asset is a federal income tax refund. Under FLA. STAT. § 735.302 (2002), a summary action to secure the federal income tax refund, not exceeding $2,500, can be taken.

Also, most, if not all, Florida probate courts will receive, with the summary administration petition, a petition to determine homestead status without additional charge.

In summary, the above-mentioned procedures point out that there are many situations in Florida where the attorney will advise not to use a living trust. However, in many situations, the purpose that a revocable living trust will provide for our client may be best to cover the following:

1. Avoid guardianship of the grantor's property, should the grantor suffer diminished capacity or become incapacitated. While this point is considered most important in living trusts, the Florida attorney must keep in mind the availability of the durable power of attorney (FLA. STAT. § 709 (2010)). While this is a viable alternative to the trust, it must be considered a second choice, especially for long-term use. The point is that in Florida, guardianships should be avoided whenever possible, as this procedure, because of misuse in prior years, has become very expensive to administer.

2. Provide for management of investments and property. This purpose becomes especially effective if a client has the desire to use a professional trustee.

3. Avoid probate. As prior comments indicate, this should not be the primary goal, but, under certain circumstances, with a surviving spouse, such may be the proper procedure.

4. Ancillary proceedings. A trustee holding title to foreign property can be very useful in the saving of time and expense regarding the transfer of title for out-of-state property.

Pointers on the New Florida Trust Code

We are currently experiencing a very beneficial enactment that has taken place in Florida with the addition of Chapter 736 of the Florida Statutes with an effective date of July 1, 2007, and with most provisions being retroactive.

FLA. STAT. § 736.0403(2)(b) (2007), of the New Florida Trust Code, is specific as to the requirement of the execution of a trust agreement; i.e.,

> The testamentary aspect of a revocable trust, executed by a settlor who is a domiciliary of this state at the time of execution, are invalid unless the trust instrument is executed by the settlor with the formalities required for the execution of a will in this state. For purposes of this subsection, the term 'testamentary aspects' means those provisions of the trust instrument that dispose of the trust property on or after the death of the settlor other than to the settlor's estate.

Note the phrase, "executed by a settlor who is a domiciliary of this state at the time of execution . . . ." This section applies to trusts created on or after July 1, 2007, the effective date of the new trust code.

For earlier executed trusts, the case of *Alter v. Zuckerman*, 585 So.2d 303 (Fla. Dist. Ct. App. 1991), is a good overview of the development of execution requirements of Florida.

Florida had a better than average trust statute in Chapter 737 (virtually all of which is now part of FLA. STAT. § 736), but in the year 2000, following the publishing of the Uniform Trust Code, the desire arose to establish a New Trust Code for the Florida practitioner encompassing much of Chapter 737, but incorporating some of the Uniform Code and adding provisions to assist in the drafting and administration of trusts in Florida. In 2001, an Ad Hoc Trust Code Revision Committee was established to codify Florida trust law. The Committee took five years to produce its final product, but it is considered to have been time wisely spent. The New Trust Code is considered more comprehensive than Chapter 737, but the Committee established FLA. STAT. § 736.0106 (2007) providing that the New Code is supplemented by the Common law of trust and principals of equity.

> FLA. STAT. § 736.0106 Common law of trust; principals of equity: The Common law of trusts and principals of equity supplement this Code, except to the extent modified by this code or another law of this state.

IMPORTANT NEW CONSIDERATIONS IN FLORIDA'S TRUST AND ESTATE...

FLA. STAT. § 736.0414 gives trustees a means to modify or terminate an uneconomic trust. This is not a mandatory provision and may be overridden by a grantor's expressed contrary provision in the trust instrument. On the other hand, if the drafter believes that the best interests of the beneficiaries will be served with termination at $50,000, this provision should be specifically placed in the trust instrument.

From the Uniform Trust Code, Florida has codified in FLA. STAT. § 736.0416, "That upon application by any interested person a court may modify a trust to achieve a settlor's tax objective." There is a provision that such modification must not be contrary to the settlor's intent. Interestingly, the code states, "The court may provide that the modification has retroactive effect." However, successful action under this section does not ensure that the modification will be recognized by the IRS for tax purposes.

The new code contains three new sections—§§ 736.04113, 736.04115, and 736.0412. All three of these sections specifically declare that they constitute an addition to and are not in derogation of common law rights to modify, amend, or terminate trusts.

Each section must be applied in the context stated; however, none of the three is applicable while the trust agreement is revocable. Prior to the new code, modification and/or termination were "accepted" by many drafters as near impossible. These new provisions open many possibilities of modification, revision, or termination, and must be carefully noted as "possible" throughout the term of the trust agreement.

It is important to point out that much of the New Code, unless otherwise stated within the code, applies to all Florida trusts.

Most Florida trust practitioners have practiced with the desire to keep all beneficiaries fully informed during the administration of the trust but there was always a question as to "who and how much" was entitled to information. FLA. STAT. § 736.0813 (2007) now requires that a trustee keep *qualified* beneficiaries of an irrevocable trust reasonably informed of the trust administration. FLA. STAT. § 736-0103(14) (2007) defines a qualified beneficiary as a living beneficiary who, on the date the beneficiary's qualification is determined:

a. Is a distributee or permissible distributee of trust income or principal;

b. Would be a distributee or permissible distributee of trust income or principal if the interests of the distributees described in paragraph (a) terminated on that date without causing the trust to terminate; or

c. Would be a distributee or permissible distributee of trust income or principal if the trust terminated in accordance with its terms on that date.

There now exist five mandatory rules of duty as to irrevocable trust:

1. Notify them of the trustee's acceptance of the trust and the full name and address of the trustee within sixty days after the trustee's acceptance.

2. Notify them of the existence of the trust, the identity of the settlor, the right to request a copy of the trust instrument, and the right to accountings within sixty days after the trustee acquires knowledge of the creation of an irrevocable trust or that a formerly revocable trust has become irrevocable.

3. Upon reasonable request, furnish them with a complete copy of the trust instrument.

4. Once a trust becomes irrevocable, furnish a trust accounting to them annually as well as on termination of the trust or on a change of trustee.

5. Upon reasonable request, provide them with relevant information about the trust's assets and liabilities and the particulars of the trust administration.

As in FLA. STAT. §§ 737, 736 allows a grantor to override a Code provision, however, with twenty-three exceptions which are listed in FLA. STAT. § 736.0105(2) (2007).

An important new provision, "Certification of Trust," FLA. STAT. § 736.1017 (2007), should be utilized by every practitioner whenever necessary or useful. This provision should terminate the need for many phone messages and letters debating the need to release copies of the client's trust.

Finally, it should be pointed out that even though the scope of the New Code can appear far reaching and, as stated, most provisions are retroactive, still there is expected to be little impact on the trusts we have already drawn in Florida.

Elements of Estate Planning

The following are among the useful elements of estate planning, based on my experience:

1. Last Will and Testament - I consider the will as most important in the first stages of estate planning, in that by its preparation I really learn "who my client is."

    a. Some of the client's personal life will be disclosed—their employment, their goals in life, together with hopes and wishes for their family.
    b. Family composition – An estate planner should be familiar with the structure of the client's immediate and extended family.

        i. Should we consider testamentary trust?
        ii. Should we consider special family member needs and/or special needs trust?
        iii. Is this a second marriage, suggesting the use of a qualified terminal interest property (QTIP) trust?

    c. Client's assets

        i. How is title to client's assets held?
        ii. Will there likely be probatable assets upon the death of the first spouse?
        iii. Is life insurance available, who are the beneficiaries, and is the necessity of an irrevocable trust a possibility?

iv. Are there specific bequests to be considered, such as family heirlooms or jewelry carrying an emotional significance to a beneficiary, or will the client be comfortable with the personal property separate writing as provided for in FLA. STAT. § 732.515 (2002).

2. Testamentary Trust – A testamentary trust is set forth in the client's will and only becomes active upon client's death. Testamentary trust literally means a "trust in a will."

I have found that testamentary trusts are primarily called for in estate planning for clients with minor children and tend to be driven primarily by the needs of the minors, but at the same time, provides a means of some control over the parents' assets and carrying out of the parents' desires for their children during their adolescent years and even early adult years. Basically, until the child is educated and mature, and capable of handling their own financial affairs.

3. Trustee – My remarks here are directed to all trustees, but emphasis is placed on the choice of a trustee who will serve in place of the spouse/trustee or following the death of both spouses.

The Florida Trust Code clearly details the trustee's duties and the major duties of a trustee. All of these should be considered when counseling with the client and drafting the trust agreement. The client should understand, before choosing a trustee, the broad and mandatory rules of the Florida Trust Code, FLA. STAT. §§ 736.0801-736.0817 (2007), and, specifically, the following sections which I have listed. Further, I encourage the client to discuss the duties and responsibilities of a trustee with the proposed trustee, or better yet, I offer to meet with the proposed trustee to discuss these duties and obligations, or I will place them in writing for the use of the client's discussion with the proposed trustee.

a. FLA. STAT. § 736.089 – Duty to Administer

Acceptance to serve a trustee establishes a fiduciary office mandating conduct of good faith and strict adherence to the trust agreement and the Florida Trust Code.

b. FLA. STAT. § 736.0812 – Duty of Loyalty

The trustee is bound to administer the trust "...solely in the interest of the beneficiary."

I believe all trust drafters should emphasize the prohibition of "self-dealing" and emphasize caution when dealing with relatives or close associates.

c. FLA. STAT. § 736.0803 – Duty of Impartiality

In administering a trust with multiple beneficiaries, careful regard must be given to the beneficiary's respective interest.

d. FLA. STAT. § 736.0807 – Delegation by a Trustee

Yes, a trustee may delegate, but is charged with exercising reasonable care, skill, and caution in doing so.

e. FLA. STAT. §§ 736.0810, 736.0813 – Duty of Record Keeping and Duty to Keep Qualified Beneficiaries Adequately Informed of Acts of Administration

No further comment is necessary on this subject, but these are two areas that trustees can easily "forget to do."

f. FLA. STAT. § 736.0809 – Duty to Control and Protect Trust Property

This probably is the first overt act of a trustee and should be immediately accomplished.

g. FLA. STAT. § 518.11 – Duty to Follow "Prudent Investor Rule"

This rule is detailed in FLA. STAT. § 518.11(1)(a)-(f). We must remember that when a testamentary trust is activated, the spouse, settlor, has died and has little influence over the trustee's actions save for the education and instructions to the trustee before he or she steps into this office of service. While there is no requirement, and probably is not binding, I suggest that the client prepare a letter to the proposed trustee setting forth client's desires and preferences.

Surely all practitioners representing trustees in the administration of a trust cover all of the above with their trustee client. My point has been to bring forth these factors before the trustee is chosen, so the client has support for his or her best choice of a trustee.

4. Personal Representative and Alternate – The general powers of a Florida Personal Representative are set forth in FLA. STAT. § 733.608 with general duties set forth in FLA. STAT. § 733.602, stating basically that a personal representative is a fiduciary and is under a duty "…to settle and distribute the estate of the decedent in accordance with the terms of the decedent's will and this Code as expeditiously and efficiently as is consist with the best interest of the estate."

The client should be urged to name an alternate personal representative, in the event for any reason the primary personal representative does not serve. Parties who may serve as personal representative in Florida are set forth in FLA. STAT. § 733.

5. Guardian – If your client has or may have children, the matter of guardianship is extremely important. What could be more important than having a voice as to who will raise your children if premature death catches both spouses?

The guardian of the person of a minor (under eighteen years of age) is an adult authorized by law to take physical control of and provide care for the minor. Florida courts grant duly appointed guardians broad authority over medical decisions and the general welfare of the minor. FLA. STAT. § 744.312(3)(c) states that the court shall consider "…any person designated as guardian in any will in which the ward is a beneficiary."

IMPORTANT NEW CONSIDERATIONS IN FLORIDA'S TRUST AND ESTATE...

Florida court decisions have made it clear that the primary concern of the court is to determine what is in the best interest of the minor. Under the above numbered statute, a family member is given preference to the appointment. However, if another is nominated in the Last Will and Testament of the deceased parent, and especially if the family members agree on the nomination, the court rarely rejects the deceased parents' choice of guardian. Before making the nomination, urge the client to first have a full and frank discussion with the proposed guardian, which includes the extent of the client's estate and the client's desires and hopes for their children.

Further, it is assumed, but inquire of the client regardless, in reaching a decision for the proposed guardian, that the client has carefully included an analysis of religion, political leanings, character, integrity of the subject parties, age, health, and will they unconditionally accept this great responsibility.

Finally, it should be pointed out that anyone convicted of a felony is prohibited from serving as guardian.

6. Durable Power of Attorney - Utilizing Florida Statute 709:

   a. Holder and alternates
   b. FLA. STAT. § 709 covers medical power of attorney and medical directive.

7. Living Will - Florida has excellent clear statutes— FLA. STAT. § 765.302-304—providing "...that any competent adult may, at any time, make a written declaration and direct the providing, withholding, or withdrawal of life-prolonging procedures in the event that such a person has a terminal condition, has an end-stage condition, or is in a persistent vegetative state..." FLA. STAT. § 765.302(1).

   Such statement "...establishes a rebuttal presumption of clear and convincing evidence of the principal's wishes." FLA. STAT. § 765.302(3).

8. Location of documents - Firm's vault for original estate planning documents.

9. I have never been able to predetermine the time required for estate planning. I am willing to put in as many hours as it takes, with the client's cooperation. My experience in estate planning finds that every client and his needs are unique.

Pitfalls and Common Mistakes

The key pitfalls and mistakes to avoid in this area include:

1. Not properly funding the trust.

   If property, tangible, intangible or real, is not properly titled in the trustee, the trust agreement will not control the asset. Such assets will become part of the decedent's residual probate estate and could pass possibly to unintentional heirs.

2. Trust agreement does not adequately set forth how incapacity is to be determined.

   In trusts, a judicial determination should not be required. Therefore, there must be a clear direction as to how a grantor is to be determined incompetent. In Florida, most feel comfortable with specifying that all can rely on the professional medical opinion of two licensed physicians. Sometimes the personal physician of the grantor is required to be one of the two physicians.

3. Failure to specifically direct the payment of fees, costs, and taxes incurred through specific devises of assets held in another state. It may well be the grantor's desire for the residuary estate to cover all such expenses. But you must be certain and, if not, clearly charge the proper asset with expenses required for its transfer to the beneficiary. Also, if devised personal tangible property requires shipping, where is the expense paid from?

4. Failure to keep in mind guardian status, such as age, health, availability, minor's changing need, and possibly minor's desire.

5. Lack of clarity in granting powers and in identifying contingent beneficiaries. It is much better to use a lot of words when giving direction than not enough.

6. Not specifying the procedure as to how a trust agreement can be amended, modified, or revoked.

7. No spendthrift clause.

8. Naming a venue of administration for the client who frequently changes location.

9. Failure to name alternate personal representatives.

10. Failure to name successor trustees.

Florida and Spendthrift Trust Provision

A spendthrift clause is designed to be an asset-protection shield, because the trustee, not the beneficiary, has the sole right of possession and control of the trust assets. One of the most common attacks addressed to pierce a spendthrift trust is to show the beneficiaries' control over the trust.

Over the years, many Florida trust drafters have been meticulous in the drafting of the spendthrift clause. This has been especially true in the "Special Needs Trust" relating to governmental financial relief programs. This is a good procedure and should be continued. For several years, I have used the following for Special Needs and Dynasty Trusts:

> If any of Grantor's beneficiaries should be disabled and receiving benefits of any nature from any governmental authority, then Grantor's Co-Trustees shall retain such beneficiary's share and it is Grantor's specific instruction that such bequest is not to be used for such beneficiary's general welfare, maintenance and education. Notwithstanding anything to the contrary contained in other provisions herein, in the event the existence of a

bequest under this trust has the effect of rendering such beneficiary ineligible for Supplementary Security Income (SSI) or assistance from the State of Florida or any other program of public benefits, the Trustee is authorized but not required to terminate this trust. The undistributed balance of said trust shall then be, at the sole discretion of Trustee, distributed free of trust to a Court appointed Trustee or Guardian of such beneficiary under such a court order that would grant full and complete discretion in the application of this devise for the special needs of such beneficiary, provided no part of the corpus of this trust is used to supplement or replace public assistance benefits of any governmental agency having a legal responsibility to serve persons with disabilities or impairments from which my beneficiary is receiving at the time of my death. No part of the principal or undistributed income of said trust estate shall be considered available to my beneficiary.

But, I point out that FLA. STAT. § 736.0502 lessens the requirements for clear validity. In fact, FLA. STAT. § 736.0502(2) makes it clear that no special language is necessary to create a spendthrift trust.

Miller v. Kresser, 34 So.3d 172 (Fla. Dis. Ct. App. 2010), may be the first Florida Appellate decision applying Florida's new tax code governing spendthrift trusts. The Trial Court found that the beneficiary held dominion over the trust because the trustee allowed the beneficiary "complete access to the trust assets" and ruled that the trust assets were subject to creditors' claims.

The Fourth DCA reversed, however, on grounds that legal and equitable title was never merged and, therefore, per FLA. STAT. § 736-0504(2), the creditor could not compel a voluntary distribution "whether or not the trustee has abused his discretion in managing the trust."

Apparently, at least for the present, in Florida, no matter how bad a trust is managed, it is the words in the body of the trust agreement that controls.

Key Takeaways

- Seeking the client's objective is foremost. In considering whether to use a trust in an estate plan, we must keep in mind that often, other options will serve the client's needs. I like to have the client tell me in their own words what they want to do for their family and heirs following their death. It then becomes my responsibility to carefully evaluate the client's desires; available assets, now or proposed; and then make recommendations as to a plan.

- The most useful elements of Florida estate planning include the client's will; durable power of attorney; living will; and location of documents.

- Mistakes to avoid include not properly funding the trust; trust agreement not adequately setting forth how incapacity is to be determined; failure to specifically direct the payment of fees, costs, and taxes incurred through specific devises of assets held in another state; failure to keep in mind guardian status; lack of clarity in granting powers and in identifying contingent beneficiaries; and not specifying the procedure as to how a trust agreement can be amended, modified, or revoked.

- Over the years, many Florida trust drafters have been meticulous in the drafting of the spendthrift clause. This has been especially true in the "Special Needs Trust" relating to governmental financial relief programs. This is a good procedure and should be continued.

Elwood Hogan Jr., a partner at McFarland, Gould, Lyons, Sullivan & Hogan PA, practices in the areas of real property law; wills, trusts and estate planning; and probate.

Before becoming partner of McFarland, Gould, Lyons, Sullivan & Hogan, P.A. in 2000, Mr. Hogan was a partner at Wolfe, Bonner & Hogan from 1964 to 1975. He was a prosecutor in the Municipal Court in Clearwater, Florida from 1966 to 1968 and president of the Florida Municipal Judges Association in 1972.

Mr. Hogan is Martindale-Hubbell AV Peer Review Rated. He is a member of the American Bar Association; the Florida Academy Professional Mediators; the Kiwanis Club (District Governor, Florida District, 1979-1980), and the Clearwater Bar Association (president, 1972-1973).

INSIDE THE MINDS

Mr. Hogan is admitted to practice before the U.S. Court of Appeals (6th Circuit), U.S. District Court Florida, the U.S. Tax Court, and the U.S. Supreme Court. He is a Certified Circuit Court Mediator.

Mr. Hogan received his B.B.A. from University of Georgia and his J.D. from Stetson University.

Advising Clients on Creating and Updating an Effective Trust and Estate Plan

Brad A. Galbraith

Partner

Hahn Loeser & Parks LLP

ASPATORE

Introduction

Given my geographical location, in Naples, Florida, my practice focuses on retirees who have a significant net worth. But because of my background as a CPA, I also often work with successful business owners who may have significant net income but more modest net worth. While my primary practice is in Naples, Florida, my firm also has an office in Indianapolis, Indiana, which is where I started my practice. In Indianapolis, my clients are generally executives or business owners, and as they retire and move to Florida, their focus and concerns change a bit, as they shift their focus from earning income to maintaining their net worth.

My background as a CPA before becoming an attorney is helpful in this area of practice because I understand the interrelation between income taxes and estate taxes and can assist my clients with both types of tax planning; therefore, I continue to maintain my CPA license, although I do not actually practice as a CPA. I am board certified by the Florida bar in estate planning, wills, trusts, and estate administration. One of the things that I think differentiates my practice from many others is I that have always tried to determine what makes estate plans fail. Rather than simply drafting documents and leaving my clients to implement the planning, I try to be proactive and avoid common planning problems before they arise. Essentially, I tend to focus on some things that many other attorneys do not necessarily put sufficient time into.

Common Trust and Estate Topics in Florida

One issue that comes up fairly often in this practice is the question of domicile. My clients are often in the process of moving from a northern state to Florida, and they are trying to sever any previous ties so that they can get out from under that northern state's estate or inheritance tax process. Therefore, a very frequent concern and issue for such clients is how they can become domiciled in Florida, and more importantly, how they can sever their domicile with that northern state so that they are not later drawn back into that state's taxing system.

Another common issue for clients in this state is the Florida homestead law. When a person is domiciled in, and owns a primary residence in,

Florida, then under the Florida state constitution, that home is considered their homestead. That distinction is important in several different contexts, including asset protection, property taxation, and estate planning, where confusion about homestead can cause the most problems. If you are married and you have minor children, you cannot simply stipulate through estate planning to whom your home should go at your death. There are restrictions under the Florida state constitution that are intended to protect your surviving spouse and minor children after your death. However, in today's world of second marriages, it is not at all uncommon to have a client come into our office and say, "We are happily married and we own a home here in Florida, which was bought with my resources. We also have a lake house back in Minnesota, which was purchased with my wife's resources. We want that home in Minnesota to go to her children at her death, but we consider the Florida home to be my home, and we want that house to go to my children upon my death." Unfortunately, I have to explain to the client that it will not work that way without very specific estate planning, including either prenuptial or postnuptial agreements.

Asset protection is an issue that comes up much more often today than it used to. I have a number of very wealthy clients who have unexpectedly found themselves in financial trouble, largely because of the significant decline in Florida real estate values. Essentially, they leveraged their real estate to buy more real estate, and because prices have come down their estates have been diminished. If real estate prices continue to fall, clients want to know how to protect themselves to the greatest extent possible under Florida law. Consequently, that is another common question in the estate planning context in Florida as well.

Protecting Assets and Retirement Accounts for Beneficiaries

In this economy, people are much more interested in making sure their beneficiaries, especially their children, are protected from a divorcing spouse or creditors once they inherit their assets. Simply put, people are not only worried about potential financial problems for themselves, but also, even more so, they are worried about their children's finances. If they pass significant assets on to their children, they want to make sure that those assets that they worked a lifetime to build up are protected.

33

Another issue that is not uncommon involves retirement account planning. Many older clients, for the most part, did not have the opportunity to put away retirement dollars on a pre-tax basis during their working years—401ks and IRAs did not exist back when my older clients were working, or at least they were new enough that they did not take advantage of them. Therefore, we are hearing a lot more questions about planning for retirement benefits among my client population, aged seventy-five and younger.

Recent Social and Economic Issues Affecting Estate Planning

Again, we are seeing an increasing number of issues in this community arising from second marriage situations; clients want to make sure that their surviving spouse is protected while still providing a substantial inheritance to their children. These complex family situations are challenging because they require the attorney to apply real problem solving and client counseling skills, and oftentimes, they require application of unique planning solutions.

Another issue that is coming up much more frequently in this economy is asset protection. Five years ago, very few of my clients had genuine, specific concerns about their financial future, because my clients are typically very wealthy people. Today, however, given the state of the economy, the uncertain financial future, and concerns about inflation, many of my clients are concerned about being able to maintain their lifestyle and still pass on their assets to their children some day in the future.

Preliminary Client Meetings

When first meeting with an estate planning client, I have them complete a confidential estate planning questionnaire where I ask about their family relationships, their past work history, and their children's financial well-being, as well as their grandchildren. I also need to find out quite a bit of information about their assets, including the cost basis as well as the current fair market value of those assets. Of course, I also want to know about any previous estate planning the client has completed so that I can determine whether their existing plan simply needs to be updated or whether the clients are starting from ground zero.

34

When people come to me for estate planning they often have specific concerns in mind; therefore, they are often quite aware of what is motivating them to see me. However, I always ask some specific questions about why the client has come to see me. They may be concerned about a health issue that was not there previously, or they may have new concerns about a child's marriage. Therefore, it is a good idea to simply come out and ask the client what has motivated them to come in and see me, because that can really shed a lot of light on what needs to be done first.

Whenever possible, I find that it is also very helpful to speak with the client's financial advisers and financial planners, including their CPA. Again, many of my clients are moving from a northern state to Florida, and many have previously been business owners. Therefore, I will often speak with their northern attorney who may have handled the sale of their business in order to find out what is going on, and what their concerns might be when the client moves to Florida.

Preliminary client meetings can be unpredictable. Rarely are my clients' situations "simple"—more often than not, my clients have children from a previous marriage, spendthrift children or grandchildren, business interests, and income tax planning issues in addition to estate tax concerns.

Advising Clients on Designing a Trust

Certainly, the design of a trust will vary considerably, based upon a client's needs. Therefore, I talk to them about whether they have family members who might make good trustees, or whether it is more appropriate to seek out professional trustees or corporate fiduciaries to fill those roles. If there are family members who can do the job, that may be fine, but sometimes when we really delve into the details, we find the family member is already overworked, overstressed, and overburdened such that the client should give serious consideration to finding a good institutional trustee instead.

One thing that I often focus on in trust planning, especially foundational revocable living trust-based planning, is proper title to the client's assets. Proper titling of assets is crucial to making a trust work properly, but unfortunately, many clients do not understand that, and the job does not get done. Typically, the attorney does not do the re-titling; the attorney makes that a homework assignment for the client—i.e., "now that you have this trust in place, you need to go back and re-title your investment accounts to your trust." The client will often agree that they will do the re-titling, but in today's world with the volume of paperwork associated with changing account titles, many clients will not get around to completing the task.

Recognizing that an estate plan is only as good as its funding, I hired a paralegal to spend her time assisting clients to take care of those asset transfers and complete the paperwork, so that we know that the job actually gets done—instead of just assigning it to the client and realizing that at least 25 percent of the time, the client will not do the job. The typical client who comes into my office has not looked at their estate plan in ten or more years; therefore, if I send them out of my office with a homework assignment that involves doing something they are not looking forward to doing—i.e., working with a financial institution to transfer their assets into a trust—the odds are that they will procrastinate like they did before, and nothing will be done. Unfortunately, if something then happens to the client, his or her family members will not be happy when it turns out that the estate plan did not work properly because the assets were not properly titled. Therefore, spending that extra time to make sure that asset titling gets done properly makes for happier clients and much happier family members—and it results in much better estate planning.

Key Elements of the Estate Planning Process

The proper drafting of an estate plan is obviously incredibly important— and fortunately, it is also fairly simple. We have a lot of software and other resources available to us to make sure that what we draft includes necessary legal language. Drafting is no longer an art form for lawyers as it was before computer technology took hold. Today, a lawyer who wants to draft particular trust provisions is likely to be able to find countless examples of similar language. Therefore, the more important part of the process for me is properly matching estate planning options with the client, particularly because we have so many options available to us. I view estate planning much like going to an eye doctor's office, where they put a funny looking contraption in front of your face and ask, "What is better for you—A or B?" and then they develop a prescription that is right for you. Similarly, estate planning involves good drafting, but the thing that sets apart a good estate plan from a boilerplate estate plan is matching the options to the client, and really educating the client about what options are available.

Therefore, when beginning to design an estate plan for a client, I typically draw a four-page long flowchart on a white board, which can be photocopied. I start by drawing the standard basic elements of an estate plan, as there are certain things that we know are going to be true—i.e., for example, there are certain documents that we know we need to do for everyone, and there are certain basic questions that must be answered. For example, who will be your disability trustee and who will make your health care decisions if you become disabled; who will make financial decisions for your estate after you pass away? Consequently, I have notations on this four-page long spreadsheet or flowchart about the questions that I need to ask. Over time, I have found that unless I have that chart in front of me, it is all too easy to make assumptions. As a result, it is much better if I consult the chart, and then take the time to educate the client about each element.

Typically, I talk about how the estate plan works if they are alive, and I make sure to point out what it does and does not do. For example, from an asset protection standpoint, foundational estate plans and revocable living trusts do not offer asset protection; yet just because the term "trust" is used, many people think that such a trust provides some sort of asset protection. Therefore, it is important to explain to the client not only what a specific trust does, but also what it does not do.

We then talk about what would happen if one or both spouses become disabled, both from a financial standpoint and from a health care standpoint, and what happens if either the husband or the wife passes away first—i.e., who takes over; who can remove a trustee; what access to the assets will the surviving spouse have; and what ability to change the estate plan will the surviving spouse have? An interesting option that clients may have never considered before is a trust provision that might say that if one spouse passes away and the surviving spouse ever gets remarried, then that spouse must execute a prenuptial agreement with certain provisions, and if they do not, then there are some consequences in the estate plan—for example, no more access to income or principal from the family trust; no more access to principal from a marital trust; or perhaps the spouse is removed as a trustee of the trust. That helps to ensure that the surviving

37

spouse will take that additional step of getting a prenuptial agreement in order to protect him or herself.

Under Florida's homestead law, unless there is a valid prenuptial or postnuptial agreement, a surviving spouse will have certain enforceable rights to the homestead, as well as rights to a portion of the estate. This is true whether the spouse has been a longtime spouse of forty years, or whether the marriage occurred a month earlier, at age eighty. Consequently, requiring a prenuptial agreement if the surviving spouse ever remarries can avoid misunderstandings many years later.

Simply put, reviewing the options available to clients when designing an estate plan results in better educated clients and more complete estate plans.

Filing and Storing Estate Planning Documents: New Technologies

As compared to some states, Florida has no filing requirement; therefore, when a trust or will has been executed, it is not usually recorded with the county court system until the person has passed away.

Therefore, when filing a trust or will in the attorney's office it is certainly a good idea to make sure that any original document is adequately protected by keeping it in a "will vault." In my practice, we also scan estate planning documents into our computer system so that they are much more easily available without always having to go to the hardcopy. Thanks to our ability to scan documents, it is much easier to keep those documents at hand, and the completed originals can be put away in a place where they do not have to be readily accessible, which keeps them much safer. Meanwhile, scanning allows estate planning documents to be easily shared with others; they can be sent to the client's adviser, CPA, attorney, and their children. Essentially, it is much easier to work with scanned documents rather than frequently pulling out originals and photocopying them, which might eventually result in a damaged, destroyed, or lost document.

Updating an Estate Plan

I have a formal estate plan updating program for which my clients pay an annual fee, and as part of that annual fee, they can request amendments at any time. However, we generally work off of a three-year revolving cycle—i.e., during the first year we take another look at the client's assets to make sure they are properly titled and the estates are properly balanced; in the second year of the updating program we update personal instructions such as tangible personal property instructions, detailed health care instructions, memorial instructions, and detailed instructions for trustees and guardians concerning children and grandchildren; and in the third year, if we have not seen the client face to face in the previous three years, we bring them back into the office for a meeting where I review a four-page flowchart depicting their estate plan, in order to remind them of what their estate plan says. I often find that given three years, people's memories will fade, and they may not remember exactly what they have done—it is not that they do not remember to whom their assets are going, but often they forget the benefits of trust planning and the protections they built into their plan.

Therefore, it is very helpful to have clients review their estate plan every three years, whether they believe they have changes to make or not. Very often clients do not think they have any changes to be made, and then they come in and upon discussion, we find that, in fact, some changes do need to be made. I find that having such a meeting once every three years is normally adequate, as long as the client knows that they can certainly pick up the phone in the interim period if they have specific concerns.

Mistakes to Avoid in Trust and Estate Drafting

Perhaps the biggest mistake that is made in the trust and estate drafting process is failure to fund the trust once it has been drafted. Having the document is one thing, but actually making it work is another. Therefore, as noted, I have a paralegal whose job it is to follow up with a client and make sure the funding process gets done. Rather than asking the client about their assets, we prepare a spreadsheet of their assets, and we note who needs to do what to get things done. Also, as part of our updating program, we go back to the client one year after their estate plan is complete and say, "The following items were on your to-do list—have you done them? If not, there is no better time than the present to finally get them done."

Probably the second most common error is the failure to update the estate plan. Again, I find that it is very common to meet with clients who have not taken their estate plan out of the manila folder for a good ten to fifteen years—sometimes back when their children were in high school, and their concerns and assets were completely different. All too often, their plan may need to be updated due to changes in financial or family circumstances or tax laws.

I always tell my client that estate planning is not a transaction. It is not as if you "purchase" an estate plan and it continues to work forever; a good estate plan requires attention. Therefore, once the client has invested their time and money to develop a well-designed estate plan, they need to be sure there is a process in place to keep it up to date with periodic checks and amendments.

It is equally important for the estate planning attorney to stay up to date in this area of law in order to assist their clients properly. To that end, I subscribe to several different services that give daily, weekly, and monthly briefings on my specific area of practice, and that tips me off to anything that might be important for me to know in my practice, and pass on to my clients.

Final Thoughts

I believe that adopting a formal estate planning updating program is the next step in the evolution of the estate planning practice. It is not only what is best for the client, but it is best for the attorney's practice also. An updating process results in much better drafted estate plans, and the formal process also keeps the attorney in contact with their clients much more often than if the attorney simply waited for the client to contact him or her again. Consequently, it is less likely that the client will move on to another attorney once an estate plan has been drafted. It also good for the attorney from the standpoint that it is not so easy to find new clients; therefore, once an attorney has a client, it makes a lot of sense to take care of that client's needs on an ongoing basis. Rather than treating estate planning as a transaction, both clients and their attorneys should think about estate planning as an ongoing relationship.

Key Takeaways

- When first meeting with an estate planning client I have them complete a confidential estate planning questionnaire where I ask about their family relationships, their past work history, and their children's financial well-being, as well as their grandchildren. I also need to find out about their assets, and I want to know about any previous estate planning the client has completed.

- One thing that I often focus on in trust planning, especially foundational revocable living trust-based planning, is proper title to the client's assets. Proper titling of assets is crucial to making a trust work properly, but unfortunately, many clients do not understand that, and the job does not get done.

- Estate planning involves good drafting, but the thing that sets apart a good estate plan from a boilerplate estate plan is matching the options to the client, and really educating the client about what options are available. Therefore, when beginning to design an estate plan for a client I typically draw a four-page long flowchart on a white board, which can be photocopied.

- It is very helpful to have clients review their estate plan every three years, whether they believe they have changes to make or not. I find that having such a meeting once every three years is normally adequate, as long as the client knows that they can certainly pick up the phone in the interim period if they have specific concerns.

Brad A. Galbraith is a partner with the firm and co-partner-in-charge of Hahn Loeser & Parks LLP's Indianapolis office. His practice focuses exclusively on providing creative, cutting-edge estate, tax, and business planning advice to business owners and other wealthy individuals. Mr. Galbraith is board certified in wills, trusts, and estates by the Florida Bar Association.

Mr. Galbraith began his professional career as a certified public accountant. After switching to the practice of law and seeing the ineffectiveness and inefficiency of traditional planning methods, he endeavored to find a better way to assist his clients with estate, tax, and business planning. As an estate planning attorney, he developed a model designed to provide clients with comprehensive, personalized estate, tax, and business succession plans that withstand the test of time.

Mr. Galbraith maintains an Indiana CPA license and is a frequent presenter on estate and tax planning topics to CPAs and attorneys at conferences and continuing education events throughout the United States. Additionally, Mr. Galbraith is the co-author of an extensive continuing education program for CPAs, which was published and distributed nationally. That program, titled Estate Planning for CPAs, has been presented to thousands of CPAs throughout the United States.

Mr. Galbraith is a member of the American, Florida, Collier County, Indiana State, and Indianapolis Bar Associations, the American Association of Attorneys – Certified Public Accountants, and Florida Institute of Certified Public Accountants. He was listed in FIVE STAR: Best in Client Satisfaction Wealth Managers, 2010.

Mr. Galbraith received his J.D. from Indiana University School of Law, summa cum laude, where he was executive managing editor of the Indiana Law Review. *He received his B.S. from Indiana University in accounting.*

Understanding Your Client's Estate Planning Needs: Creating the Right Strategies

Leslie J. Barnett and Sara A. Tolliver

Partners

Barnett, Bolt, Kirkwood, Long & McBride

ASPATORE

Introduction

We primarily practice in the areas of federal and state taxation, and wills, trust, and probate administration. The firm was established in 1975, and we have developed a firm of excellent lawyers. Eight of our attorneys have LL.M. degrees in tax law, and many of them sub-specialize within discreet areas of taxation. For example, we do a lot of work in the estate and gift tax area, while other lawyers in the group specialize in pension, controversy work, charitable planning, and mergers and acquisitions. In addition to estate and trust administration, we also do guardianship administration, and have been involved in what is referred to as special needs or supplemental needs trusts. We also do transactional work dealing with business issues.

Key Trust and Estate Topics in Florida

The key issue that we are facing in this practice area this year—and it is not necessarily limited to Florida—is the repeal of the federal estate tax and the generation-skipping tax, and the uncertainty about what is going to happen with this tax in the future. The repeal will sunset at the end of this year if the U.S. Congress does not act. Florida's estate tax will be reinstated as well. This will have a big impact on our client base. Many of the estates we administer have not been taxable estates in the past because the unified credit equivalent was $3.5 million in 2009. If the credit reverts to $1 million instead of $3.5 million, it will affect many of our clients.

Another key concern in this area pertains to the administration of trusts. At this point in time, there are many issues regarding the generation-skipping tax and what effects the repeal has on the funding of trusts during this year. For example, if a gift is made to an irrevocable generation-skipping trust in 2010, should the donor's generation-skipping transfer tax exemption be allocated to such gift? If there is no allocation of the exemption, will a future distribution from the trust be subject to generation-skipping tax? We are waiting for guidance from the IRS on these issues.

Yet another estate planning issue that is affecting everyone in Florida is exemplified by recent cases that deal with the new methodologies of reproductive births—i.e., egg donors, sperm donors, and surrogate mothers. Neither the judicial law nor the legislatures have been able to keep up with the trends in reproductive medicine in terms of who is entitled to inherit through a will or trust—in other words, does a lineal descendant include someone who was born due to artificial insemination and born through a surrogate mother? These areas need further explanation.

2010 Estate Tax Issues

At the present time, we are waiting to see what Congress will do with respect to the federal estate tax. Because Congress failed to re-enact the 2009 levels of exemptions and tax rates, we will probably see a huge jump in the estate tax brackets next year. Many people are also very concerned that Congress may enact an estate tax law that would be retroactive to January 1, 2010. Many persons died in 2010, whose estate would have been taxable under the 2009 law. By enacting legislation on a retroactive basis there will be challenges based on the constitutionality of such a law. The litigation to resolve the issues would extend for many years and create a great deal of uncertainty.

Initially, we thought that we would have clients lining up at the door trying to make gifts this year at a time when the gift tax is only 35 percent, or that they would be transferring assets into an irrevocable trust for a younger generation while there is no generation-skipping tax in place. However, many of our clients are fearful to do so because Congress may enact some type of law in the near future that would cause that transfer to be subject to a much larger tax.

The uncertainty regarding the retroactive reinstatement of the estate tax has caused some issues with respect to the administration of estates. For example, a surviving spouse may want to disclaim her interest in certain assets in her spouse's estate so such assets may pass to other beneficiaries, tax free. However, the surviving spouse is concerned that the estate tax may be reinstated retroactively. Therefore, the surviving spouse may wait until the very last minute to make a qualified disclaimer, simply because she is concerned that if she disclaimed her interest any earlier she would be unable to use the marital deduction if the estate tax was retroactively reinstated. Consequently, when administering estates for such clients, we are taking a "wait and see" approach with respect to when a disclaimer should be filed.

We are also encountering basis step-up issues with respect to our clients' estates this year. Under the current law, there is a carryover basis for assets that are inherited, with certain limited exceptions. For example, someone with up to $1.3 million worth of assets will receive a step-up in basis for those assets. If they pass the assets to a spouse, there would be a step-up in basis to the fair market value of the assets at the person's date of death up to $3 million of value. Also, there is a new Internal Revenue Code provision that requires the filing of a return with respect to the allocation of the step-up in basis. However, although there have been some guidelines with respect to what should be on the return, a sample form has not yet been released. If you have an estate with a fair market value in excess of $1.3 million—or $3 million if you have a spouse—then an issue arises as to which assets are going to be stepped up, and which are not.

A fact-finding problem within this area pertains to assets that have been held for numerous years; in such cases, it can be difficult to find information on what the basis in the assets were for the decedent. In 1976, Congress passed a law regarding carry-over basis for such assets. However, dealing with this law became intolerable for the working public and their CPAs. In many cases, decedents had passed away without leaving any records concerning their assets; therefore, a carry-over basis could not be found. Fortunately, a few years later Congress repealed the carry-over basis rules retroactively to the date of enactment.

Educating Clients about Estate Law Changes

We have debated about whether or not to send out alerts to our clients about these estate tax issues, and ultimately we chose not to, simply because we do not know what is going to happen in this area. Therefore, we have been answering questions as they arise—and frankly, very few clients are asking many questions about these issues, much to our surprise. Interestingly, the publicity attendant to the recent deaths of some very wealthy people with multi-billion dollar estates, including Dan Duncan and George Steinbrenner, has created outrage in some circles, due to the fact that the government lost out on a great deal of money because of the hiatus in the estate tax.

New Issues for Trust and Estate Clients in Florida

Increasingly, many of our clients are concerned about setting up trusts for children that may have certain personal issues, such as problems with handling money or a drug or alcohol problem. In some cases, they are concerned about their children's creditors, or they are not happy with the child's selection of a spouse. As a result, we are seeing trusts being set up for longer periods of time; in other words, the client's assets are being held in trust until their children are older.

We are also seeing an increased utilization of pre-marital agreements by younger people. In many cases, their parents have been successful and accumulated wealth, and the parents are concerned that their children are going to lose that wealth in their first divorce. Therefore, they are imposing a pre-marital agreement requirement on their children. In some cases, they look to control the actions their children take by leaving their inheritances in trust with an independent trustee who will make decisions as to timing and amounts of distributions, but pre-marital agreements remain a popular strategy as well.

The Impact of the Economy on Trusts and Estates Law

We represent high net worth individuals whose portfolios have been severely affected by the recession, but not to the point where the imposition of a transfer tax would be eliminated. I have not seen any particular slowdown in estate planning, except perhaps for the insurance industry. When the estate tax exemption was $7 million for husband and wife there were fewer estates subject to the estate tax, and thus, less need for liquidity at death, thus less need for life insurance. At this time, the liquidity need at death has diminished, but this need will increase next year when the estate tax exemption reverts to $1 million per decedent.

I believe that the estate planning area has been somewhat affected in recent times due to the unknown climate with respect to the estate tax and generation-skipping tax. At the same time, more people have been inquiring about asset protection—and I believe that trend is not only tied to the state of the economy, it is also tied to the litigious nature of our society. No one wants to take responsibility for their own actions; therefore, they seek to impose responsibility on a third party—and they often do that by suing. In some bankruptcy cases, for example, a debtor's assets have been structured in a manner so as to be exempt from the claims of creditors. Consequently, many clients are finding that they can either walk away from their debts with impunity, or negotiate more strongly with their creditors to keep a larger amount of their assets if a judgment is entered.

Key Concerns of Surviving Family Members and Beneficiaries

The biggest concern of surviving family members and beneficiaries is generally money. There will always be an estate planning client that wants to avoid probate administration because of the perception that the probate process is extremely expensive (which it usually is not). Most surviving family members and beneficiaries want to know how quickly we can administer the estate and when their funds will be distributed to them.

In some cases, there will be family disputes surrounding an estate, and in other cases there is harmony. However, we face few family disputes in our practice, because we stress the importance of estate planning to such an extent that the client's death is almost a legal non-event (although emotionally affecting). The transition has already been orchestrated because the planning has been worked on for many years. Business succession planning is a very important area. You do not want to have a situation where a family's income-producing business transfers into the hands of siblings or descendants who operate the business going forward, but exclude other family matters because of control issues. In these situations, a fight usually arises because someone does not get what they think they are entitled to.

Our client base has aged dramatically, but most of the clients' wealth is held primarily in real estate, or they are the owners of closely held businesses or executives of publicly held companies that made their wealth because of the stock market. However, we are seeing more multiple or second family situations these days, which requires some unique planning because you are dealing with clients who have children from multiple marriages or a blended

UNDERSTANDING YOUR CLIENT'S ESTATE PLANNING NEEDS

family situation. In blended family situations, we may use a trust for the surviving spouse. Upon the surviving spouse's death, the assets then pass to children from a prior marriage.

Preliminary Client Meetings: Gathering Information

At our first client meeting, we try to establish a financial baseline for the client. Essentially, we create a balance sheet that shows the approximate value of the client's assets—although we need to know that for tax purposes—but more importantly, how the assets are held.

For example, are the assets jointly held or held in the client's name alone? Are they in a trust, an IRA, an annuity policy, or life insurance? From a tax perspective, we want to know what the impact would be if all of the client's assets were transferred either under the laws of intestacy or as a result of operation of law, or what the tax implications would be if everything went to Aunt Tillie as opposed to Uncle Saul. Most importantly, we ask the client what they want to see happen with their assets, and then we try to reflect those wishes in the best tax vehicle that we can possibly devise.

The probate process and the importance of titling are topics that we discuss with clients early on in the estate planning process. Even though you may set up a will and trust combination, the goal is to put many of your assets in trust so that you can avoid the probate process and its attendant delay in transferring assets to beneficiaries. Most importantly, the client needs to ensure that they have not made a beneficiary designation that would not be in harmony with what they actually want to happen in their disposition plan. For example, we have administered estates where the client wanted their assets held in trust until a child reached a certain age, but then they used the beneficiary designation in their IRA or life insurance policy in such a way that the child would inherit the assets outright. Basically, they did not understand how the beneficiary designation worked, and how it could erode their intent. Therefore, we always take time to educate the client on these issues, although we are realistic enough to know that they are not going to remember all the details. Hopefully, however, if they are revisiting their estate plan a few years later, they will think twice about whether they are making a new beneficiary designation correctly, and give us a call before they do so. Simply stated, we always try to incorporate education in the

49

estate planning process to help the client in the future as they acquire different assets.

Estate Planning Mistakes Made by Clients

Unfortunately, we are seeing more instances where clients have tried to do estate planning on their own, and those plans often end up in probate. For example, we recently handled a case where the estate holder's will was drafted using an Internet form; they wanted to leave their house to one child but the will was not executed properly, and it was void. As a result, the estate passed by the law of intestacy—and now the Florida law decides how the property passes, not the decedent. In another case the estate owner knew that it was important to have a trust and he wanted to avoid probate, but he did not do a will in conjunction with the trust and did not title anything in the name of the trust, so the estate assets passed by intestacy.

Also, in Florida we have a unique constitutional provision dealing with what is called homestead property; and you have to be an expert to understand how property in Florida can be disposed of under that law, as we will explain later in this chapter. In fact, lawyers oftentimes do not get it right, much less a layman.

Choosing the Right Trust

In a simple estate plan, we create a basic trust that is amendable in combination with what we refer to as a pour-over will. This trust structure is for state purposes; it has no effect for federal tax purposes until death. Essentially, this trust structure is used for the disposition of assets and is a will substitute. It is particularly useful in cases of incapacity rather than seeking appointment of a guardian. As the estate plan and tax planning becomes more complex, we may use other trust structures.

One significant trust structure is an irrevocable life insurance trust, which cannot be changed. An irrevocable trust holds life insurance outside of the gross estate, for the benefit of either the surviving spouse or some other individual, usually the children. We may also use an Intentionally Defective Irrevocable Trust (IDIT) in conjunction with transferring closely held

UNDERSTANDING YOUR CLIENT'S ESTATE PLANNING NEEDS

businesses to the next generation at a discounted value, or a Qualified Personal Residence Trust (QPRT) for moving the future appreciation of property outside the gross estate; this can be done for a principal residence or a secondary residence, such as a vacation home.

We also create all types of charitable trusts, including charitable remainder trusts and charitable lead trusts, which create deductions at death by holding assets in trust for a charitable purpose. We also create grantor retained annuity trusts whereby the grantor retains an interest in the trust for a number of years. GRATS can be an effective estate freeze technique whereby appreciating assets are removed from the grantor's estate at a lower transfer tax cost.

We also create special needs trusts for individuals who are disabled, which can generally be established by a third party or self-settled. We have several clients who have children or relatives with a disability, and they are obviously interested in protecting their assets so that they can be used for the special needs of that disabled individual, and yet the individual will not be considered as owning the assets. Therefore, they can still apply for certain governmental benefits, because these children or relatives are often not able to get insurance that is affordable.

In addition, we create self-settled special needs trusts in conjunction with a disabled person's personal injury suit which trust will receive a structured settlement, a lump sum, or some combination. It should be noted that there is a payback provision to the state for funds that are expended on behalf of a disabled person by the state, but during their lifetime, the funds that are in the trust can supplement their needs, therefore giving them a better quality of life.

The Estate Planning Process Timeline

We often tell our clients that doing estate planning is like eating an elephant—you cannot do it in just one bite; it requires small bites over time. Simply put, estate planning continues for the rest of your life; you can commence the process with our firm by doing a basic will and trust, and then continue with the planning process for at least a year—keeping in mind that a good estate plan should be tweaked each year thereafter.

One issue that can hold up the estate planning process is lack of knowledge—i.e., if the client does not know their assets, their value, their income tax basis—or if they cannot make up their minds about certain issues. Problems can arise if the wife wants one thing to happen and the husband wants another thing to happen, particularly when they have children from different marriages and children from their existing marriage. We have had clients who cannot decide who to designate as guardian for their minor children.

In other cases, you will meet with the client and give them drafts of an estate plan, and then they will sit on their documents for a period of time. We may continue to remind the client that, even if they want changes made in the future, they should execute the basic will and trust that has been prepared, rather than allow their assets to pass by intestacy.

There is a well-documented phenomenon that many people believe that doing estate planning is going to cause their death, which is why they do not want to address the issue, and even when they finally overcome that fear and come in to talk about an estate plan, they may not complete the process for that very reason. Some people who are planning a vacation also have a belief that they are more likely to die in a plane or a car crash, and that will prompt them to create an estate plan.

With respect to updating an estate plan, we always tell our clients that if there is any major change in the law that will affect them or our general client base we will send them a reminder to come in to update their estate plan. Also, if some major life cycle event occurs in their life, then they should contact us. Even if neither of those events occur, we let the client know that we should always meet at least every five years to review their current plan.

Unique Aspects of Florida Trust and Estate Law

The most unique aspect of Florida trust and estate law, as previously noted, is homestead property and related issues. There are limitations, both under the state constitution and statutorily, that limit how you can devise your homestead. For example, if you have a surviving spouse and no minor children, you can only leave your home to your spouse outright; you cannot

UNDERSTANDING YOUR CLIENT'S ESTATE PLANNING NEEDS

leave it in trust for her. If you have a minor child and a spouse, then the spouse may utilize the homestead during her lifetime (a life estate), and the decedent's children receive a vested remainder interest. Alternatively, if the property is held as a "tenant by the entirety" with a spouse, that is not a homestead for devise purposes. In other words, if you decide to hold the house jointly with your spouse, it would obviously pass to him or her—whoever the survivor is—by operation and law, and the homestead rules would not apply. These rules become important in estate planning. For example, if someone holding the homestead in their individual name states that they want to leave it in trust, first for the benefit of their spouse and then to pass to his children from a prior marriage, that is not a plan you can put in place unless the spouse waives her homestead rights.

Other parts of the homestead law deal with exemptions for each individual homeowner. For instance, there is an exemption of up to $50,000 on the value of a home for property tax purposes, and there is a cap wherein your ad valorem taxes cannot be increased more than 3 percent per year. We often run into issues with the cap and the exemption when we are working with a qualified personal residence trust—typically when the property is coming out of the trust after a period of years. Fortunately, some administrative code provisions and statutes allow us to assist the client in this area.

For example, let us say that the parents who have put their home in a qualified personal residence trust want to continue to live in it for a ten-year period, after which time title to the property will pass to their children. However, when the property transfers to the children it triggers a tax re-assessment. Therefore, we have found that if we allow the parents to remain in the house as a tenant under a ninety-nine-year lease from their children, then even if the home is re-assessed after the initial transfer it will still have a $50,000 exemption from property tax, and a new 3 percent cap would be applied going forward.

Another issue in relation to homestead property, in addition to exemptions and the limits imposed on real estate tax increases, is creditor protection. Simply stated, there has been some recent case law to the effect that if you put your homestead in a revocable trust that you would not get creditor protection. For example, there is a case in the First District Court of

53

INSIDE THE MINDS

Appeals in Florida that basically says that homestead property in revocable trusts are not exempt from the claims of creditors, and therefore, they lose their constitutional homestead protection, *In re Basonetto*, 271 B.R. 403 (Bankr. M.D. Fla. 2001), although there are other cases that have decided the issue differently. *Engelke v. Estate of Engelke*, 921 So.2d 693 (Fla. Dist. Ct. App. 2006), *In re Edwards*, 356 B.R. 807 (Bankr. M.D. Fla. 2006). The recent *Olmstead* decision (*Olmstead v. Federal Trade Commission*, 2010 WL 2518106 (Fla. 2010)), for instance, deals with whether or not a charging order is the sole remedy for creditors when imposing their judgment rights against an individual who owns shares in a single member LLC. The Court in *Olmstead* held that a court might order a judgment debtor to surrender all right, title, and interest in the debtor's single member LLC to satisfy an outstanding judgment.

Finally, there is a statute concerning elective share rights of a surviving spouse, which is handled differently in Florida than it is in other states. Florida does not have a graduated step-up as to percentage based on the length of the marriage; we have a standard 30 percent share of what is called an "elective estate." Therefore, in many cases—especially in second marriages if there is no prenuptial or postnuptial agreement that addresses this issue—the spouse will establish what we call an elective share trust. In that trust, we can use a formula to limit what the surviving spouse would receive under the elective share statute—and this can add some complexities and complications to a trust or will drafting.

Common Errors in Trust and Estate Document Drafting

Unfortunately, it seems that a number of lawyers have not learned how to write a proper trust or estate plan; the language as drafted is often very ambiguous. We have found that you must be very precise in your drafting so that forty years from now, when someone picks up that piece of paper, they are able to understand what was intended by the testator. Of course, it is preferable if, after the death of the testator, you can get all the beneficiaries to agree on what was the intent of the estate plan, but if an estate plan is not drafted properly, you may have to go before a court and try to get a declaratory judgment as to what certain terms in the plan documents may mean. Sometimes the conflicts that arise have to do with tax issues or with what property is supposed to pass to what beneficiary.

54

UNDERSTANDING YOUR CLIENT'S ESTATE PLANNING NEEDS

The second big problem that we see in this area relates to the titling of assets. Sometimes clients make the mistake of titling an asset as jointly held with a right of survivorship, expecting that their trusts will be funded at their death. The asset passes by operation of law in a manner different from what was anticipated solely because of improper titling. Unfortunately, many people do not understand that titling can be very important. When you initially meet with a client they may have a certain list of assets, but obviously as time goes on that list will change—they will acquire different assets or change their assets, and that is where titling can destroy their estate plan. In some cases, the client does not even realize that they made a beneficiary designation or titling that ruins what they had planned to do in their will or trust.

Historically, lawyers have utilized estate plans as a loss leader, but I do not recommend doing that. Simply put, you should charge for your time and your expertise as you do for any other matter, because clients are fickle. Historically, you were a client's lawyer for life, and if you did their will, their family would come to you to probate their estate or advise them with regard to trust issues. However, today, we are finding that is no longer the case. Sometimes one client will have six different lawyers from six different firms, and utilize them for different matters, depending on the lawyer and their areas of expertise. Therefore, you should always charge for your services, while also making sure to be ethical and do your very best job.

Helpful Resources

In order to keep on top of issues in this practice area we subscribe to RIA Checkpoint, the BNA Portfolio series, CCH and Westlaw, and numerous periodicals such as *The Journal of Taxation*, trusts and estates magazines, and other periodicals. Our lawyers are members of the Real Property, Probate, and Trust Law Section of the Florida Bar, and the Tax Section of the Florida Bar, which publish periodic newsletters that are of great benefit.

Looking to the Future

The Florida estate tax was repealed before 2010, when the federal system changed the estate tax imposed by the various states from a credit to a deduction. Essentially, you received a deduction from the adjusted gross

55

estate for what you actually paid the state when computing the tax due the federal government. If the federal estate tax returns, it will probably become a credit again. Therefore, Florida estates will again be subject to Florida estate tax.

Also, because of the devaluation of real property in Florida, the revenue for the state is severely depressed. Historically, the number one fundraiser in Florida is the sales tax, and secondarily, it is real property tax, and as property values go down, tax revenue goes down. Therefore, it is possible that we will see an enactment of some tax laws in the state that could affect our clients tremendously—maybe even some form of value-added tax. We already have local county tourist taxes that levy a sales tax, which pushes the tax rate from the standard 6 percent to as high as 12 percent in some counties. With the tourist industry depressed due to bad press from the Gulf oil spill, we have seen a reduction in state revenue from tourism dollars.

Final Thoughts

An attorney in this practice area needs to stay on top of the changes that are taking place, because the actions Congress takes can repeal your education on an annual basis. It takes a tremendous amount of dedication to succeed in this practice area. You need to be sensitive to the emotional needs of your clients, as well as being aware of the law itself. The estate planning process involves serving in more of a counselor position as opposed to a legal position. You are helping people in a very sensitive area; most people care about who gets what from their estate and how they get it—therefore, you cannot approach these issues coldly.

Most importantly, you need to get to know your client and their extended family. As you talk to them, you may discover that they have a relative who has a special need, and they may need to make provisions for that disabled relative. Unfortunately, in some cases a client winds up totally disinheriting a child because their attorney did not realize that they could have set up a special needs trust. Therefore, even though you may not be specializing in a particular area, you should at least have enough education in that area to recognize that an issue exists and there may be another way to address it. You do not want to create a plan that makes a client's relative ineligible for government benefits simply because the client has left them money—which

UNDERSTANDING YOUR CLIENT'S ESTATE PLANNING NEEDS

is why it is so important to ask the right questions so that you know those issues are out there.

Fortunately, there are law school courses in estate planning that can help younger attorneys develop the necessary skills in this area, including being empathetic to their client's needs. For instance, I remember that the first advice that Jerry Manning gave me during an NYU estate planning course was to put chairs in your office that rock and swivel, because your clients are going to be tremendously nervous talking about death. Young lawyers should take courses taught by people who have "been there and done that." Also, if you belong to a large firm where you can be mentored by an older lawyer, that is great; if not, you should seek out the tax section or the wills, trusts, and probate sections of your local bar association in order to gather some tips from the older lawyers. Simply put, if you are not in a firm where there is a mentor, find someone who is willing to mentor you; they may be in another firm, or in a local bar association that offers mentoring programs.

Key Takeaways

- At our first client meeting, we try to establish a financial baseline for the client. Essentially, we create a balance sheet that shows the approximate value of the client's assets—although we need to know that for tax purposes—but more importantly, how the assets are held. Most importantly, we ask the client what they want to see happen with their funds, and then we try to reflect those wishes in the best tax vehicle that we can possibly devise.

- With respect to updating an estate plan, we always tell our clients that if there is any major change in the law that will affect them or our general client base, we will send them a reminder to come in to update their estate plan. Also, if some major event occurs in their life, then they should contact us. Even if neither of those events occurs, we advise the client that we should meet at least every five years to review their current plan.

- It takes a tremendous amount of dedication to succeed in this practice area. You need to be sensitive to the emotional needs of your clients, as well as being aware of the law itself. The estate planning process involves serving in more of a counselor position as opposed to a legal position.

- Young lawyers should take courses taught by people who have "been there and done that." Also, if you belong to a large firm where you can be mentored by an older lawyer, that is great; if not, you should seek out the tax section or the wills, trusts, and probate sections of your local bar association in order to gather some tips from the older lawyers.

Leslie J. Barnett is a partner at Barnett, Bolt, Kirkwood, Long & McBride. He practices in the areas of estate planning; probate and trust administration; federal income, estate and gift taxation; excise, state, and local taxation; charitable giving and exempt organizations; administrative tax controversies and tax litigation; real estate transactions; corporate, partnership, and trust law; and mergers and acquisitions.

Mr. Barnett has been listed in The Best Lawyers in America *in the areas of trusts and estates, tax law, and non-profit/charities law for twenty-six consecutive years. He has been named Florida Legal Elite (Wills, Trusts & Estates) by* Florida Trend Magazine. *Chambers USA named him as one of America's Leading Business Lawyers, Tax & Estate Planning and he has been named a Florida Super Lawyer (Tax) from 2006 to 2010.*

Mr. Barnett is a member of the American Bar Association (Tax Section), the Hillsborough County Education Foundation (Professional Advisory Committee), the All Children's Hospital Foundation (Professional Advisory Committee Member), and the Tampa Bay Community Foundation, Inc. (Professional Advisory Committee). He is also a member of The Florida Bar and Florida Institute of Certified Public Accountants where he is a lecturer on tax matters. Mr. Barnett is an adjunct professor of law at Stetson University College of Law

Mr. Barnett received his B.A. and J.D., with honors, from the University of Florida *and was executive editor of the* University of Florida Law Review. *He received his LL.M. in taxation from New York University.*

Sara A. Tolliver is a partner at Barnett, Bolt, Kirkwood, Long & McBride. She is also a certified public accountant. Ms. Tolliver's practice is primarily dedicated to estate planning, tax planning, estate and trust administration, as well as general business and corporate matters.

Ms. Tolliver counsels individuals and families in estate planning matters, including income, estate and gift tax planning, business succession planning, and prenuptial and postnuptial planning. She is experienced in drafting complex trusts, wills and other estate planning instruments. Ms. Tolliver also assists families with disabled children or relatives and prepares special needs trusts. She represents family members and professional fiduciaries in the administration of estates and trusts, including postmortem planning and preparation of estate tax returns. She also represents clients with respect to IRS audits and examinations, specifically federal estate tax audits.

As part of her business practice, Ms. Tolliver assists clients with commercial agreements, such as supply and service agreements, operating agreements, and shareholder agreements. She also represents clients with respect to stock and asset sales and acquisitions.

The practice of law is Ms. Tolliver's second career. Prior to earning her law degrees and joining the firm, Ms. Tolliver was a store manager and employee of a major electronics retailer for over fourteen years. Ms. Tolliver's experience in retail management gives her a unique and informed perspective with respect to the needs of her business clients.

Ms. Tolliver is a member of The Florida Bar (Tax Section), the Florida Institute of Certified Public Accountants, the Hillsborough County Bar Association, the Tampa Bay Estate Planning Council, and The Partnership for Philanthropic Planning of Tampa Bay.

Ms. Tolliver received her LL.M. in taxation from the University of Florida, her J.D., with high honors, from the University of Florida, where she was management editor of the University of Florida Law Review, *and her B.S. from University of South Florida and Indiana University.*

Dedication: *To all who have gone before us – we learn from our mistakes.*

A New Outlook on Trust and Estate Planning Strategies for Florida Clients

Helen S. Atter
Partner

Matthew T. Harrod
Attorney

Wood, Atter & Wolf PA

ASPATORE

Common Trust and Estate Topics in Florida

At the present time, the biggest trust and estate topic in Florida seems to be asset protection due to the economy. With individuals losing their jobs or having investments in real estate go bad, they are trying to protect their assets in order to not lose everything they have built up to this point.

Other common issues that are brought to us by clients are probate avoidance (i.e., because the client just had to probate a family member's estate), asset protection for their children, and special needs planning for children so that (i) the children do not lose eligibility for their benefits and (ii) they still have some other money to live off of to be able to enjoy life.

The Impact of the Economy on Trust and Probate Issues

The economy has drastically affected clients and their need for estate planning, both for themselves and for their beneficiaries. Some clients who were once in an estate taxable situation no longer are and need to simplify their planning. Other clients are more worried not about themselves but their beneficiaries and how they can protect their inheritance from the beneficiary's creditors. The economy has shown that estate planning is not necessarily only for the rich and famous.

Clients are also more cognizant of the fact that probate in the state of Florida is a very tedious process which takes a lot of time due to Florida statutes requiring a ninety-day creditor waiting period and money in legal and other fees. However, with proper planning, probate can very easily be avoided.

Preliminary Client Meetings

When a new client seeks our help, we first try to find out exactly what the problem is. Without knowing the problem, we cannot give them an answer. Sometimes clients come in with what they think is a problem, but ultimately, it ends up that something else really is the problem. Therefore, clearing up the issues is the first thing that must take place.

The information that we seek will depend on the situation, but we always ask for personal information, family information, and asset information. It is always important to speak directly to the client. Sometimes we will also have to speak with the client's CPA and financial adviser to get specific tax and business information in order to fully understand the entire situation.

Developing Client Strategies Regarding Trusts

We always set out a clear agenda at the beginning of the client meeting that includes data gathering, education, and then recommendations. We gather data (personal, family, and assets information) but also review the client's current estate planning documents. Based upon the information we have collected and what their documents say, we then educate them in tax law and property law. As long as they know those two areas of the law, we feel they will understand our recommendations and why we are giving those recommendations.

We typically design the trust using a three-page template we have created. The template walks the client through the different stages of their trust's life from while the client is alive through (i) what happens upon the client's disability, (ii) what happens upon the client's death, and (iii) if married, what happens upon the surviving spouse's death. The design template takes anywhere between ten to thirty minutes to complete.

The strategy itself is always the same: data gathering, education, and recommendations. The questions though are usually different based upon the answer to the questions mentioned in the preceding paragraph.

Typically, the terms of the trust change depending upon the beneficiaries involved (spouse, minor versus adult beneficiaries, special needs beneficiaries, etc.), the assets involved (for example, whether there an IRA or 401(k) involved), and for married clients, whether this is their first, second, third, etc., marriage.

These factors are important because they directly influence the terms of the trust. If a beneficiary has special needs, the trust created for that beneficiary must include language to prevent the beneficiary from losing their current government benefits. If the client is married but on their second marriage, the trust created for the surviving spouse may need to have an independent third party trustee to prevent the surviving spouse from withdrawing all of the assets and leaving the children from the client's first marriage without an inheritance. These are only two of the many reasons the strategy of data gathering, education, and recommendation is so important.

Choosing the Right Trust for the Right Client

By far, the most common types of trusts that we deal with are the revocable living trust and the irrevocable life insurance trust.

The revocable living trust is a will substitute that allows a client to dispose of their assets upon their death without having to go through probate and allows a client to do disability planning without having to rely upon a power of attorney. So no matter what, the client should have a revocable living trust as a foundation to their estate plan.

If the client has a taxable estate, there are many different ways to lower or eliminate their estate tax bill. Our recommendation depends on what their tastes are for life insurance or how complex an estate plan they are willing to work with. The easiest way to deal with the estate tax is through the irrevocable life insurance trust, also known as an ILIT. It is a separate trust, which is irrevocable, that purchases a life insurance policy on the grantor/grantors of the trust. Then upon the grantor's death, the death benefit is used to pay the estate tax bill. The benefit of this trust is that the death benefit of the insurance is not included in the grantor's taxable estate.

Key Elements of the Estate Planning Process

We believe that the most important element of the estate planning process is the education element. Most clients come into a meeting with an estate plan, but they have no clue as to what it says and why. Therefore, we think that it is very important both for the client relationship and client retention that they know exactly what we are doing and why.

The other important element of the estate planning process is keeping the estate plan up to date. Studies show that about 70 percent of Americans have no estate plan. However, those that do have an estate plan only update it every 17.2 years. Life, law, and lawyers change a lot in 17.2 years. A way of combating the lack of updating an estate plan is to implement an annual maintenance program where the clients are notified annually of any changes in the law that may affect their estate plan. This ensures that the clients are thinking about their estate plan on an annual basis, even if only while they are reading the letter.

Differences between the Estate Planning Process and the Creation of a Trust

The estate planning process is really all about the talking, educating, learning, and planning aspect of the estate plan. The creation of a trust is more of the detailed and drafting aspect of the estate plan. While both are important, we believe the estate planning process is vital—otherwise, the trust may mean nothing to the client and probably will not accomplish their estate planning goals.

Unique Regulations, Practices, and Laws in Florida Trust and Estate Law

One trust and estate law that is unique to Florida is the homestead laws in Article X, section 4 of the Florida Constitution. Essentially, if the clients want to distribute their homestead in a certain way upon their death, especially in second marriages, then a postnuptial agreement needs to be drafted so that there is not a cloud on title later on when a beneficiary attempts to sell the property. Under Florida law, the homestead must go to the surviving spouse, either outright, as a tenants in common owner or through a life estate. However, if the client wishes for the home to go directly to their children, then both spouses must sign a postnuptial agreement waiving their respective rights to the homestead upon their death. This will not affect any other homestead protections against tax increases and asset protection; it just allows the client to pass the homestead on to individuals other than the surviving spouse.

Updating an Estate Plan

We meet with clients to update an estate plan as often as they would like to do so. We send out an annual letter letting clients know of the changes in

65

the law. If the client feels, based upon the changes in the law, that they need to make a change or even discuss a change in their estate plan, they can then meet with us to discuss any possible change. We would ideally like to see the client every three to four years to discuss any possible changes to their estate plan. By ensuring the estate plan is up to date, the estate plan is less likely to be challenged upon the death of the client.

Common Errors in Trust and Estate Drafting

We find that the names that appear in a trust and estate plan often tend to be in error. Many attorneys are using the cut-and-paste approach to drafting an estate plan, and are therefore leaving the wrong names in the document from a previous estate plan they drafted.

We have seen a lot of erroneous tax planning as well, especially because there is no estate tax in 2010. This will cause a tremendous amount of litigation if not corrected, because the surviving spouse, absent a prenuptial or postnuptial agreement, cannot be disinherited in Florida. Florida and a few other states have enacted laws that are in place specifically in 2010 to allow a court to revise a trust where the current tax laws would cause a spouse to be disinherited. However, many of these laws expire after December 31, 2010.

Another common error is that the beneficiaries of life insurance, retirement plans, and annuities are incorrect. If someone passes away with incorrect beneficiary designations, there is little that can be done to correct that after death. It is very important to review a client's beneficiary designations when creating or updating their estate plan.

Finally, the biggest error we find in trusts is the fact that they are not funded. Funding is the process of re-titling assets so that they are in the name of the trust and not jointly or individually owned. Most attorneys do not fully fund the trust. Some do not mention it at all – possibly because they are unaware of the resulting problems, or possibly so that they get the probate work upon the client's death. A trust has no power over assets that it does not own and will cause a probate to get the assets into the name of the trust. A pour-over will is used to transfer the assets to the trust after death through the probate process. The pour-over will does not avoid probate.

The client may not be affected by these errors because the document may not come into play until after their death. However, the client's beneficiaries will be affected, either by being left out of the plan or having to wait as the plan is modified by the court. Further, the client's beneficiaries will have to pay higher legal fees if the erroneous tax planning causes them to litigate and/or probate the estate. Fortunately, all of these errors are easily (and usually cheaply) avoidable by keeping the estate plan up to date.

The Impact on the Attorney

The attorney who makes mistakes in the trust and estate planning process could be subjected to a malpractice claim. A recent case out of New York, *Estate of Saul Schneider v Victor M. Finmann*, 15 N.Y.3d 306 (N.Y. 2010), allowed a personal representative to sue the estate planning attorney for planning in regards to a life insurance policy. Most states allow some malpractice actions by estates and beneficiaries against attorneys for estate planning negligence.

The attorney's reputation among his peers could be negatively affected as well. A number of clients come to attorneys from other attorney referrals. If an attorney does not completely meet the needs of a client, the referring attorney will be much less likely to refer any future clients to them.

In order for lawyers to avoid making these common mistakes, it is important to keep up on education, be a member of an estate planning council, and have others to bounce ideas off of. Also, by having an annual communication with the client, when the client comes back in, the lawyer will be better able to serve the client due to the experience they gained in the interim.

Challenging Aspects of Trust and Estate Law in Florida

Florida's biggest challenge is how to deal with the homestead of the decedent as was discussed previously. Otherwise, Florida has the same challenges in the trust and estate law area as most other states have, including simply getting the client to do what you ask them to do. The best approach to tackling these challenges is education of both the attorney and client.

Changing Areas of Trust and Estate Law

The area of trust and estate law that is changing the most is tax planning, because the law is not settled as to where the estate tax exemption will be in 2011. Although it is well settled that the estate tax will return to a $1 million exemption at a 55 percent rate for anything above that, it is also assumed that Congress will act to create a new exemption that will be retroactive to January 1, 2011.

Helpful Resources

In order to stay up to date in this area, lawyers should consult listserves, WealthCounsel, blogs, Leimberg Services, and attend continuing legal education seminars. We closely monitor listserves and Leimberg services on a daily basis to stay up to the minute on changes to any area of the law that may affect our clients.

Looking to the Future

From all indications from a few insiders, Florida may start to sway toward a more creditor-friendly state compared to its current debtor-friendly status. Creditor lobbyists are convincing lawmakers to make certain assets, which currently are non-probate assets, into probate assets. Further, Florida is working on a self-settled trust to provide some asset protection for the trust settler. However, negotiations have caused this trust, once approved, to be so watered down that it will not be as valuable a tool as it should be.

Recently, the Florida Supreme Court issued a ruling in the *Olmstead* case that allowed a judgment creditor to obtain the membership interests of a single-member LLC. The ruling left open the possibility that the ruling could be used against a multi-member LLC as well. Prior to this ruling, the sole remedy against a member was a charging order, which only gave the creditor the right to any distributions made from the LLC but gave the creditor no control of the LLC. The creditor could not force a distribution to be made. Therefore, they may never receive anything. This change in the law devalues the LLC in Florida, because the charging order is no longer the sole remedy. For asset protection purposes, a client will now have to use a different state's LLC, such as Wyoming, to ensure that the charging order is the sole remedy.

A New Outlook on Trust and Estate Planning Strategies...

In response to these challenges, clients may need to seek other asset protection techniques that are offered by other states. In response to the LLC specifically, the Wyoming LLC is the oldest LLC in the U.S., and we will be using it more often now in estate planning because of the fact that a charging order is no longer the sole remedy in Florida. We will approach these new changes and challenges as we always do—by educating the client.

Cases, Statutes, Regulations

Cases that are relevant to the matters covered:

- *Olmstead v Federal Trade Commission*, 2010 WL 2518106 (Fla. 2010). Just released on June 24, 2010 but can be found at http://www.floridasupremecourt.org/decisions/2010/sc08-1009.pdf
- *Estate of Saul Schneider v Victor M. Finmann*, 15 N.Y.3d 306 (N.Y. 2010)

Key Takeaways

- When a new client seeks our help, we first try to find out exactly what the problem is. The information that we seek will depend on the situation, but we always ask for personal information, family information, and asset information. It is always important to speak directly to the client. Sometimes we will also have to speak with the client's CPA to get specific tax and business information in order to fully understand the entire situation.
- Based upon the information we have collected and what their documents say, we then educate the client in tax law and property law. As long as they know those two areas of the law, we feel they will understand our recommendations and why we are giving those recommendations.
- In order for lawyers to avoid making common mistakes, it is important to keep up on education, be a member of an estate planning council, and have others to bounce ideas off of. Also, by having an annual communication with the client, when the client comes back in, the lawyer will be better able to serve the client due to the experience they gained in the interim.

Helen S. Atter, *an A.V. rated attorney, is a graduate of Florida State University (B.A., cum laude, English literature, 1976) and the University of Florida Fredric G Levin College of Law in Gainesville, Florida (J.D., 1980). She is a member of the Florida Bar and Middle District of Florida.*

Ms. Atter joined the firm of Wood, Atter & Wolf PA in 2010. Ms. Atter is the managing partner of the Ponte Vedra Beach office which serves clients in the areas of business formation and transactions, corporate matters, tax, estate planning and probate, sports and entertainment law, intellectual property, licensing, consumer, bankruptcy, and civil and commercial litigation.

Prior to joining the firm, Ms. Atter spent twenty-two years with the PGA TOUR. With almost thirty years of legal experience, Ms. Atter has represented and been engaged in a variety of businesses. After four years in private practice, she was counsel and president of First American Title Insurance Company of Jacksonville, where she was responsible for the business and legal needs of offices in Jacksonville, Orange Park, and Palm Coast, Florida. At the PGA TOUR, she served as associate general counsel, vice president of human resources, and vice president of corporate compliance. For the past twelve years, although still with PGA TOUR, she was general counsel and vice president of business and legal affairs for the World Golf Foundation, which includes the World Golf Hall of Fame, The First Tee, and GOLF 20/20. In these capacities, Ms. Atter handled the day-to-day and long-term business and legal needs of these sports organizations. Ms. Atter currently serves on the boards of THE PLAYERS Championship Village, Fleet Landing, and Women In the Golf Industry.

Matthew T. Harrod *is a graduate of the University of Toledo (B.B.A., business management – cum laude 2000), Ohio Northern University College of Law (J.D., 2004), and the University of Miami School of Law (LL.M., 2005). He is a member of the Florida Bar. Mr. Harrod joined the firm of Wood, Atter & Wolf PA in 2010. His areas of practice include estate planning, probate, guardianship, and tax-related items.*

After graduation from the University of Miami School of Law, Mr. Harrod worked at The Andersen Firm, which provided estate planning and legal services to a broad base of clients in multiple states. With The Andersen Firm and with Wood, Atter & Wolf, Mr. Harrod presented frequent lectures and seminars on a wide array of estate planning and tax issues. In addition to his responsibilities as a lecturer and presenter, Mr. Harrod also maintained a full caseload. Through hard work and an extensive knowledge base, Mr. Harrod served clients throughout the state of Florida and co-counseled with firms out of state to serve the needs of additional clients. Mr. Harrod's passion these days is estate planning and tax-related issues for high-worth individuals and companies.

Creating the Right Estate Plan for Your Clients in a Growing Practice Area

Brian V. McAvoy

Partner

Harter Secrest & Emery LLP

ASPATORE

Introduction

My law practice is concentrated in estate planning, estate administration, and probate litigation. The term "probate litigation" includes disputes over estates, will contests, and will and trust construction proceedings.

Uncertainty about the Estate Tax

The major issue that estate planning lawyers face today is not a Florida issue, it is a federal issue—i.e., the future of the federal estate tax. We are currently in a very strange period of time, because there is no estate tax for persons who die in 2010. Simply put, the federal estate tax and the generation-skipping transfer tax (GST tax) do not apply to persons dying in 2010 and to GST transfers made in 2010 under the "2001 Tax Act" (a shorthand reference for the "Economic Growth and Tax Reconciliation Act of 2001"). It is possible that Congress will enact a law that will apply retroactively back to January 1, 2010.

The elimination of the estate and GST tax is only for calendar year 2010. If Congress does *not* enact a new law in 2010, the federal estate tax and GST tax will be back with a vengeance next year. In 2011, the law will revert back to the law that existed *before* the passage of the 2001 Tax Act. This means that the federal estate tax exempt amount will be $1 million, significantly lower than the $3.5 million level applicable in 2009. A reversion back to the 2001 law would be unfavorable for many people. In short, the amount exempt from federal estate tax would decrease and the tax rate would increase. Since 2001, experts in estate planning almost uniformly said that some kind of fix would be made to the law prior to 2010—that Congress would never let the estate tax disappear for one year, only to reappear a year later at a much more aggressive rate. It looks like the experts were wrong.

Unless Congress takes some kind of action on January 1, 2011, the estate tax exemption will only be $1 million and the maximum tax rate will be 55 percent. Therefore, a major issue that our clients are struggling with is how to plan for that upcoming change. There are numerous proposals going back and forth in Congress aimed at trying to get some resolution to this issue, but nothing concrete seems to be happening, which is frustrating to my clients and to many people in this practice area. The ongoing uncertainty about the federal estate tax makes estate planning a very difficult thing to do at the present time. There is also uncertainty as to whether Congress will enact a law that will apply retroactively to January 1, 2010. We are currently handling several estates of individuals who died in 2010 where the beneficiaries are anxious to receive their inheritances, but they cannot be paid because we are unsure whether there will be a retroactive tax law.

Tax Advantages of Florida Domicile

Florida is a very attractive state to live from the standpoint that Florida does not have an income tax. Indeed, our constitution prohibits the imposition of an income tax on individuals. Also, Florida has no estate or inheritance tax. Many states, northern states in particular, have an estate or inheritance tax. In addition, property taxes on Florida residences tend to be lower than they are in northern states. Therefore, Florida is a very popular place for people to relocate; in fact, we are seeing people who typically spend just a few weeks or months in Florida during the winter now thinking about whether they should become Florida residents. Florida used to have an intangible tax, which was an annual tax levied on a resident's stocks and mutual funds. That tax was a disincentive for some people to become Florida residents, but the state abolished the intangible tax in 2007. Simply put, Florida is a very attractive state to live in from a tax perspective.

The Florida Trust Code

Florida enacted a new trust code in 2007. The new code provides more protections and greater rights to beneficiaries of trusts—but that also means that there are more responsibilities and burdens on trustees of trusts. Therefore, in my practice, I am increasingly seeing cases where a trustee— particularly if it is an individual who is the trustee, rather than a bank or trust company—is not complying with all of the trustee's obligations under the law. As a result, I predict that this is going to be an area where we are going to see more lawsuits. Beneficiaries are going to realize that they have certain rights, and they are not getting the information and accountings that they are entitled to, and consequently, there will be more friction between beneficiaries and trustees of trusts.

73

Key Concerns for Surviving Family Members and Beneficiaries in Florida

What makes the estate planning practice area so interesting is the fact that you are talking to people about their family dynamics and matters that are extremely important to them. With a new client, it may take several meetings before the client feels comfortable discussing their concerns. Many of the people that I counsel tend to range in age from forty to ninety, and most have been very successful in their careers. But it is not uncommon for successful parents to have issues with their children, who may not be enjoying successful careers or have significant personal problems, such as marital or domestic problems or substance abuse issues. These kinds of issues can touch anybody's family. All of my clients love their children, but not all of them are sure what they should do in terms of their children's inheritances. They want to do the right thing, but sometimes inheriting a great deal of money can cause problems—for example, a child may inherit so much money that they will not have the incentive to be successful and work hard.

Another common theme that I have been seeing in my practice is related to the downturn in the economy. Some clients, who once thought they were affluent, are not feeling that way anymore because of the collapse in the stock market. A few years ago, they were worried about how to give money to family and charities while reducing their tax liability, and now they are more concerned about whether they will have enough money to take care of themselves for the rest of their lives.

Another common issue is clients with children who have financial problems—they may be upside down on their mortgages, or they have lost their jobs and now need mom and dad's financial help. These people are not in their twenties, but in their forties or fifties, and it is a source of concern to their parents, which sometimes calls for some changes to be made in their estate plan. For example, I have a client who wanted to leave a significant amount of money to a son, who is having severe creditor issues. The client wanted his son to receive his inheritance outright. However, I explained to the client that on the day his son receives his inheritance, his creditors may wind up seizing it. Therefore, the solution for this client is not to leave the inheritance to the child outright, but to put it into a trust with a spendthrift provision so that creditors cannot access it.

Consequently, some of the planning that I am doing at the present time seems to be less tax-driven, because we do not really know what is going to happen with the estate tax. Rather, it seems to be focused on family dynamics and problems that people are having financially because of the bad state of the economy, or other social issues.

The Initial Client Meeting

When I first meet with a new trust and estate client I try to find out why they are coming to see me—i.e., what is on their mind, and what is their family situation? My goal is to help them develop a plan that will give them peace of mind. Some clients come to me and say, "I need to do estate planning," but they do not know what is involved in the process, and they are only doing it because their accountant or financial adviser has told them they need to do it.

Therefore, I usually try to explain to the client that they have to think about a few issues before creating an estate plan. Two main issues that should be on the client's mind are: "What will happen to my assets when I die; and what kind of planning do I need to do to make sure I am taken care of while I am alive?" Clients often overlook the fact that there may come a point in their lives when they are not able to handle their financial affairs and they will need to allow other people to do that, and that entails putting powers of attorneys and revocable trusts in place. Essentially, there should be a mechanism in place so that others can take care of the client's finances while they are alive, and distribute what is left after they pass away.

Advising a Changing Client Base

New clients are often individuals who are changing their residency to Florida. Such clients used to be in their sixties and seventies, but I have recently had some new clients who are only in their forties and fifties. They are going to sell their family business and move to Florida. I am amazed at the number of people who are changing their residency just to enjoy some of the tax advantages of living in Florida.

When working with clients who have children who are not minors—typically college students or people in their early twenties—I will encourage those clients to make sure that their children have done some basic estate planning. For example, the children should have health care surrogates, living wills, and powers of attorney running to their parents so that in the event there is an issue with the child—e.g., they become sick or disabled—we would not have to have guardianship appointed for the child. Once someone is eighteen they are not a minor anymore, and they are free to do things on their own—but that also means that their parents do not necessarily have the legal authority to do things on behalf of their child. For example, after the horrific shooting incident at Virginia Tech in 2007, parents of some of the victims had a difficult time finding out what was going on with their children who were injured in that attack, and had difficulty obtaining pertinent medical information from hospitals treating their children because of the health privacy laws. However, if the child had designated his or her parents to be his or her health care surrogate, the parents would then have the right to speak to their physicians and get access to what would otherwise be confidential, protected health information.

Working with the Client on Creating an Estate Plan

Sometimes people will call me and say, "I need a trust"; and I will ask them why they think that is so. Again, some people think they need a trust because someone else told them that they need one. Therefore, before I meet with a client I typically send them a simple questionnaire that asks about basic family and financial information.

I then ask the client if they have ever done any estate planning, and if they have, I ask to obtain copies of existing documents. Sometimes the client's need for estate planning may be quite minimal because they have done extensive planning in the past, but if they have not done any previous planning, we will need to start from scratch. I usually have an initial conference with the client, and if they are married, I insist that both spouses come in. Sometimes the husband or wife who made the appointment will want to come in to see me alone and tell me "This is what my spouse wants." However, I will tell such a client that is impractical, and you cannot do estate planning that way. Therefore, if I am representing a married couple, I will insist on meeting both of them. I will ask about their family, their situation, and their assets. I will also ask what they would like to have happen if the husband dies first or if the wife dies first, just to get an idea of what their concerns are. Other key questions include: Do they have dependents? Are they charitably inclined? Who do they want to administer their estate?

I always tell my clients that regardless of whether they are very wealthy or do not have much money, they need to decide who is going to handle their estate after their death. Is it going to be a financial institution or a family member—and if it is the latter, is that person appropriate? Not only do they need to select a fiduciary, but also, if they have minor children, they will want to designate someone to be the guardian of those children in the event they die before their children reach adulthood.

We also discuss the various ways you can leave property to people after your death. Sometimes you can do an outright distribution, and sometimes you can leave an inheritance in trust for someone. A simple situation would involve a husband and wife who have two or three grown children; everyone is healthy and financially well off, there are no other issues, and the couple just wants to make sure that everything goes to their children. However, in reality, most families' situations are more complicated. For example, it is not unusual to be dealing with a married couple who have children from prior marriages. They may refer to all of the children as "their children," but when you ask them more questions, you find out that you are dealing with stepchildren. There are also many clients who are in long-term relationships and have been using the same last name for years, but they are not legally married. Such situations add a layer of complexity to the estate planning process, and you need to make sure that the planning you are doing is appropriate.

Common Misconceptions about Trusts

It is not unusual for clients to be confused about the purpose of a trust. That is understandable because there are many different types of trusts and purposes served by trusts. Sometimes you are using them for estate tax purposes—i.e., you want to minimize estate taxes, so you will use a trust designed for that purpose. Grantor retained annuity trusts, life insurance trusts, and qualified personal residence trusts are all designed with a specific purpose in mind, and it is generally the minimization of estate taxes, which is done by getting property out of your estate at a reduced transfer tax amount. Typically, these types of trusts are for high net worth clients who are engaging in sophisticated estate planning.

When explaining the purpose of a garden-variety trust to a client, I tell them that a trust is simply a mechanism for controlling an asset. A trust separates legal ownership from beneficial ownership. For example, if you have minor children, you will want to make sure that they are protected if you die and that they inherit your estate—but you may not want the children to get their hands on the money and spend it foolishly. Therefore, you need a trust to make sure that someone else is going to be controlling the money for the child's benefit. Simply put, if you are no longer here to say "no" to your child's requests for money, you need to designate someone else to fulfill that role—and that is your trustee, which could be a financial institution or a trusted friend or adviser.

The terms of a trust can be as simple or as complicated as the client wishes, and are based on what is appropriate under the circumstances. Someone might want to have a trust for a child that has very sophisticated terms— i.e., there will not be any distributions unless the child is gainfully employed, is drug free, etc. We have had trusts where the distributions were tied to the amount of income earned by the beneficiary; essentially, the more money the child earned at their job, the more money they would get from the trust.

A problem that, unfortunately, is too common is if a new client has an existing trust that they never really read or understood. It may be that the trust was designed for a certain set of circumstances, but it was not really a match for the client; and therefore, it was just not appropriate.

Consequently, creating a trust is not simply a matter of going to the shelf and pulling out a trust form. Rather, you need to talk to the client and find out as much as you can about their personal situation and goals, and then based on that information you can decide what kind of planning the client needs. For example, if your client is an elderly man who has a very modest estate and just one child, a daughter who is in her sixties, that client will likely need just a simple will that leaves everything to his daughter. For such a client, trusts and other complicated estate planning would not be appropriate.

78

CREATING THE RIGHT ESTATE PLAN FOR YOUR CLIENTS...

Essentially, the need to create a trust is a subset of estate planning. Most clients who have never done any estate planning need at least three documents—a will, a power of attorney, and a health care surrogate—but whether or not your client needs a trust depends on his or her individual circumstances. Also, a trust does not have to be a "stand-alone" document. A trust can be created under a will. Whether you should have a trust will also depend on who your beneficiaries are. Individuals who are too young or are otherwise not capable of managing significant sums of money should receive their inheritance in a trust.

The Importance of Gathering Information

Perhaps the most important element of the estate planning process is getting information from the client—which can be a challenge because people are busy, and sometimes people are not inclined to share important information with their lawyer. There is also sometimes a reluctance to talk about their family situation, which can involve issues that are rather emotional. However, you cannot fix a problem unless you know the problem exists—you will not know the problem exists until you talk to the client long enough and draw all pertinent information from them.

For example, I recently had an experience where a client came in to go over their estate plan, and after about fifteen minutes, he decided that everything was fine. We then started talking about more general topics; I asked about his kids, and he started telling me a few things about what was going on in his family. At that point, I told him that the plan we had discussed might not be appropriate, and therefore, we should do some other type of planning in case something were to happen to the client. Those key issues did not come up until the client gave me an overview of his whole situation, and I knew enough about what was going on with his family that I could make the proper recommendation. Therefore, you really have to be able to willing to spend the time with your clients in order to get to know them and draw key information out of them.

The Estate Planning Timeline

Typically, after the initial meeting with a client we can get the basics taken care of, including what kinds of estate planning documents they need. I will then try to get the documents out to the client within a couple of weeks to review, and if they are acceptable, I almost always insist that they come back in to sign the documents. It is important to make sure that the documents are signed properly—i.e., that there is the requisite number of witnesses present and that the documents are properly notarized. If the client is located a great distance from my office, I will sometimes send them instructions for signing the documents on their own. But I prefer that clients come in to my office to sign their documents.

Unfortunately, in some cases a client procrastinates about signing their estate planning documents. Some clients equate estate planning with going to the dentist—people do not really like to think about it or do it, although they know they should. Therefore, they just put it off. Also, there are clients who cannot make all the decisions they need to make. In such cases, I will say to the client, "Given the fact that you still cannot figure out exactly what you want to do, let's put a plan in place now that gets you 80 percent of the way there, and then we will tweak it as time goes on and your situation changes, or after you have had a chance to think things over and make additional decisions." For example, the client might say, "Look, I want to leave some money to my niece, but I don't know if I want to leave her $10,000 or $20,000"—and then they will not sign their will or trust because they cannot make a decision about a single detail. However, I will say to such a client, "Well, if you don't sign anything then nothing you want to have happen will happen. Therefore, let's get everything in place and put a number on what you want to give to your niece, and we can easily change it later on."

Simply put, it is important to get the basics to the estate plan in place. It is like building a house; every house needs a foundation and walls. Similarly, everyone needs a will, a power of attorney, and a health care surrogate. Some clients might need more than that; they might need a revocable living trust, a trust to benefit children or grandchildren, or an insurance trust. Depending on what their financial situation is, they may want to do more extensive estate planning in order to maximize the amount of wealth they can pass on to the next generation, protect their assets from creditors, divorce, etc. Again, there are basic estate planning documents that everyone needs, and there are more sophisticated and elaborate planning strategies if circumstances warrant it.

80

CREATING THE RIGHT ESTATE PLAN FOR YOUR CLIENTS...

In any case, you need to spend as much time on the estate planning process as it takes. On occasion, a client will know exactly what they want; they are very organized, and when you send them documents, they review and sign them right away. Alternatively, other clients are indecisive and agonize over making decisions. Therefore, no two circumstances are very much alike. In some cases, I have clients who are easy to work with because their situation is much like my personal situation, or their situation is similar to others I have encountered. In that case, I can tell them exactly what they need, but that is a rarity. In most cases, you have to work to get information from your clients, help them make decisions, and then implement those decisions in their estate planning documents.

Florida Filing Requirements for Trust and Estate Documents

In Florida, while you are alive, your estate plan is nobody's business but your own. Therefore, if you want to create a revocable trust or will, power of attorney, or health care surrogate document, you can do so, and then both the client and I will keep a copy, which is private, and nobody knows about it.

Where the filing requirement comes into play is with respect to a will. Once someone dies, Florida requires that you file the original will with the Circuit Court of the county that person lived in within ten days after their death. Also, you may need to have the will probated, which is the formal process of not only filing the will but getting a court order declaring that the will is the valid last will and have a personal representative appointed to administer the estate. Once a will is filed it is a public record—anybody can go to the court and review it. Some clients hate the idea of that; they do not want anyone to know what their will says. Those clients need to have both a will and a revocable trust, and that trust will be the vehicle that will give out their assets at their death. The pour-over will is basically a document that says, "When I die, any assets that are in my individual name at my death should be transferred to my trust." The trust does not get recorded with the court. Such a trust is important for someone who is very concerned about privacy in that it enables them to keep their estate plan private; their will can still be filed and be a public record, but it will not say anything of any great significance.

81

Maintaining Records

In most instances after we do someone's estate planning documents I always instruct them that the originals be kept in a secure location. Clients typically ask us to keep the originals, and we have a fireproof vault for that purpose. Some people want to keep the originals, and in that case, we tell them to keep the documents in a safe or a bank safety deposit box. In any event, after the client signs the documents we will have a copy in our file, and put the originals in our vault. We will also scan the signed documents to a CD, and we keep that CD in an offsite location with the idea that if our building ever burned down, the fireproof vault melted, and everything was lost, there will still be a copy of the signed document, electronically stored in an off-site location.

We also have an internal database that shows what documents we have on file for a particular client, and after the assignment is over, we docket all of our estate planning files for sending out review letters. For example, if I did an estate plan for a client in July 2010, then in July 2013 that client would get a letter from me saying, "Dear client, three years ago we did these documents for you; please review them and make sure they are still appropriate, given your circumstances."

It is also important to keep your clients' addresses up to date. In some cases, it may be that they have moved away, gone to another lawyer, and had another set of documents done, in which case we will send them their old ones and close out the file.

Unique Restrictions in Florida Trust and Estate Law – Homestead and Personal Representatives

One estate planning legal concept that is unique to Florida is the Florida homestead law. Basically, if somebody is a Florida resident, their residence is called a homestead. Alternatively, if you do not live in Florida but you buy a house or a condo there, that is your seasonal residence, and it will not be considered your homestead unless you change your domicile to Florida.

Florida homestead law has three applications. First, homesteads are given certain protections against creditors. Second, homesteads are given preferential treatment with respect to real estate taxes. The third application, which I will discuss, are the restrictions on what a Florida resident can do with his or her homestead property at death.

I have seen a number of practitioners make mistakes when they are drafting wills or trusts where one of the assets that is being affected is a homestead. The problem is a will or trust will contain a provision that violates Florida homestead law—and when that happens, you can have unintended consequences. Such mistakes are made simply by virtue of the fact that unless you specialize in estate planning in Florida, you are probably not going to be sufficiently familiar with all the intricacies of the homestead law. It is not unusual for a Florida homeowner who was living someplace else before they moved here to still use their lawyer up north—a lawyer who is not familiar with the homestead law because they do not have the homestead law restrictions in their own state, and therefore, they wind up drafting documents that contain mistakes.

Another regulation particular to Florida pertains to who can be your personal representative under your will and administer your estate. In Florida we have a restriction as to who can serve as personal representative. You cannot simply pick anybody to be your personal representative—it has to be a Florida financial institution, a spouse, blood relative, or someone married to a blood relative. A client might say, "When I die I want my wife's brother to be my personal representative," but that person is not eligible to be a personal representative in Florida. Similarly, I had a client who wanted his longtime financial adviser from Chicago to handle his estate when he dies; the client has a revocable trust, and his adviser is going to be the successor trustee. However, I told the client that unless that person is a Florida resident at the time of his death or Florida law changes, his adviser would not qualify as a personal representative. His adviser can serve as trustee, but not a personal representative.

Will and Trust Contests

Many laypeople do not realize how difficult it is to contest a will or trust. There are only three ways of doing so. First, you have to show that it was not signed with the requisite formalities—e.g., it was not signed in the presence of two witnesses, or the witnesses did not sign the document or the witnesses were not in each other's presence and in the presence of the

83

testator when the document was signed by the testator. Such problems might arise in the case of a homemade will, or a will that was not signed under a lawyer's supervision.

The second ground for contesting a will or trust is if the person did not have the mental capacity to sign the document; in other words, the person was confused, he or she did not know the objects of their bounty, or how much property they owned. You do not need to have a high level of mental capacity to sign a will or trust, but you need to know who your family is and the people you are leaving your property to, and have a general idea of what your assets are.

The third ground for contesting a will or trust is because it is the result of fraud or undue influence. If the will is procured by fraud or the undue influence of a third party, then it can be set aside on that basis—although it is difficult to prove undue influence.

The concept of undue influence covers the situation where a person's decisions are being controlled by unfair pressure and persuasion by a third person. A will that is the product of undue influence can be set aside because it was not the result of a person's voluntary act—it was the result of undue pressure and influence being exerted by a third party.

When I get calls from people who are upset over a will or trust, the usual scenario is that a family member has been disinherited by a relative whose estate they always expected to inherit, and they feel it is unfair. In such cases, you have to explain to the client, "In America, you can disinherit your kids if you want, and you can do it for a good, bad, or no reason at all." Whether it was "fair" for the decedent to disinherit someone is almost never a relevant issue. I recently had a client who had three children, and it was clear there was one child to whom she did not want to leave anything. The client was afraid that the child could contest the will, but I told her that she was perfectly capable of making the decision to disinherit the daughter. The daughter could try to contest the will later on, but she would not prevail, because there was no legal basis for contesting the document. Therefore, it is more difficult to contest a will or trust than most people think—which is a good thing, because if it was easy, then estates would be contested all the time and they would never get administered.

Mistakes to Avoid

As mentioned above, some of the biggest mistakes in this area pertain to violations of the homestead law. Another area where I often see problems is where the estate planning documents are technically correct and proper but the plan provided for in the documents is inappropriate under the circumstances. This often comes up in the case in a second marriage, where a husband wants to make sure that at his death his assets are held in trust for his second wife, but he also wants to make sure that when his second wife dies that his money ultimately goes to his children. He does not want to leave his money directly to the second wife, because when she dies she will leave it to her kids, not his kids. The husband may therefore decide to leave his money in a trust. Leaving the estate in a trust for a wife is a good idea. But in some cases the provisions of the trust cause problems.

For example, we had a recent case where the trustee of the trust for the second wife was the decedent's son, and the son and the stepmother did not get along at all. The decedent's documents said in effect, "I want to put my assets in the trust and I want my son to be the trustee, and the only beneficiary of the trust, during her lifetime, is my second wife. When she dies, the rest goes to my son, the trustee." In this case, there was nothing wrong with the estate plan documents; the son was qualified to be a trustee, and the trust provisions were appropriate. However, the mistake that was made was the decedent's selection of his son to be the trustee for his stepmother; he did not want to give her anything out of the trust, and she could not stand dealing with him. This situation could have been solved by making a bank or third party a trustee of the trust and/or by making some portion of the estate payable to the wife outright, and leaving the rest in trust.

I will often look at a client's documents and ask them, "Do you know what happens under these documents when you die?" My clients are smart and educated people, but they will very often look at me and say, "No." Unfortunately, trusts and wills are usually not reader-friendly; therefore, it is important to explain the result to the client and ask if they are happy with it. If not, I will say, "Let's see how we can fix it, and create a plan that you will be happy with."

On rare occasions, thankfully, people will come into my office with documents that they prepared on their own. For example, several years ago I met with a potential client who wanted me to draft a deed for a house to go into his trust. I asked to see the trust; he said he would not give it to me. I then asked who set up the trust; he said he did it himself, and I refused to draft the deed because I did not know what the trust said. All too often, the mistakes I see that occur in this area are not because people did not do any planning; rather, they did planning but it was not appropriate, done improperly, or was not well thought out.

Strategies for Avoiding Problems and Misunderstandings

If an estate plan concerns property in another jurisdiction, or if the clients live in another jurisdiction, it is important to get a lawyer who is licensed in that jurisdiction to help you create the plan. Therefore, if a lawyer for a client who has property in Florida is not a Florida resident, they should get a Florida lawyer to help them.

A second key strategy in this area is to read estate planning documents carefully—make sure you understand what they say and make sure the client understands them as well. Sometimes you have to sit down with the client and explain to them in layperson's terms how the documents work, make sure they understand how the plan will work, and then ask them if that is what they want to have happen. In some cases, you have to take the bull by the horns, and if you think there is a problem with the plan you should say, "Look, if I were you, I wouldn't be happy with this plan, and here is why." Sometimes you have to persuade people that they should make changes, because the plan that they have in place is not appropriate.

Helpful Resources

In order to stay up to date in this area we subscribe to a number of estate planning journals and treatises on estate and gift tax. In addition, all of the lawyers at my firm go to continuing legal education (CLE) programs, a practice which is required by the Florida bar; if you are board certified in wills, trusts, and estate law in Florida, you have to attend twenty-five hours of high quality CLE each year.

CREATING THE RIGHT ESTATE PLAN FOR YOUR CLIENTS...

We are also on all of the various listserves and blogs, and we subscribe to newsletters that keep us up to date. In my firm, we are fortunate in that we have a sophisticated trust and estates department, and we have regular internal conferences where we discuss various practice issues. We review the forms that we are using on a regular basis, and try to decide what changes we need to make in our practice. In addition, we jointly work on newsletters to send out to clients on various issues. Such activities keep you sharp, and help you maintain the high quality of your practice.

Looking to the Future

I do not foresee any upcoming changes with respect to trust and estate law in Florida. I think this is a good time to practice this area of law, although it is certainly a challenging time. Despite how bad things are in the economy—and the Florida economy has taken a hit in the last couple of years—I still think Florida is going to continue to be an attractive state for affluent people to have as their domicile for tax reasons. Also, the baby boomers generation is continuing to retire, and I think we are going to see more people from that age group retiring and moving to places where the weather is nice—and Florida is usually high on the list.

What is ultimately going to happen with the estate tax remains to be seen, but eventually Congress is going to take some action, and when that happens, people will start going back to their lawyers and reviewing their estate plans. A lot of people are currently holding back on doing estate planning until they see what happens with the estate tax law, but once action is taken, people will stop procrastinating—and in the next couple of years people who work in this area will be very busy.

Certain states have recently created what are often called self-settled creditor protection trusts. This is basically an estate planning technique where you can put your assets in a trust and still benefit from the trust, yet have that trust out of the reach of any creditors you might have. This is an attractive estate plan for people in high-risk professions, including surgeons and other people who are concerned about being sued. Alaska, Delaware, Nevada, and some of the states have approved these kinds of trusts. Florida has not—at least not yet. Looking ahead, it remains to be seen how the Florida courts will treat these self-settled creditor protection trusts that have

87

been set up in other states with respect to any property that might be located in Florida. In other words, will the Florida courts honor trusts that have been set up under the laws of other states? The second question in this area is whether there will be any push to have the laws changed in Florida so that you will be able to do those kinds of trusts under Florida law. This is an unsettled area.

Final Thoughts

In my experience, most law school students do not give much thought about becoming an estate planning lawyer. Law students tend to be too young to think about estate planning as a career path and are likely to be more interested in trial work—the type of lawyers they see in action in the movies or on television. Most lawyers migrate to this area after they have been in the practice of law for some time, which is what happened to me. I think the next ten years is going to be a very good time to practice this area of law; the law seems to be in flux, but there is a large cohort of people who are going to be needing estate planning services in the near future, as previously noted. Therefore, this is going to be a very busy and challenging practice area in the coming years.

In addition, people are living longer these days, but we are also seeing a lot more people who have incidences of dementia and Alzheimer's. These are clients who simply cannot handle their legal and financial affairs. As practitioners, we need to determine how we are going to be able to assist those kinds of clients; we need to make sure that we are taking care of our clients who cannot take care of themselves anymore.

Key Takeaways

- Creating a trust is not simply a matter of going to the shelf and pulling out a trust form. Rather, you need to talk to the client and find out what their situation is and what their interests are, and then based on that information, you can decide what kind of planning they might need to have.
- Perhaps the most important element of the estate planning process is getting information from the client—which can be a challenge. However, you cannot fix a problem unless you know the problem

CREATING THE RIGHT ESTATE PLAN FOR YOUR CLIENTS...

exists—and sometimes you do not know the problem exists until you talk to the client long enough and draw it out of them.

- If an estate plan has to do with property in another jurisdiction, or people who live in another jurisdiction, it is important to get a lawyer who is licensed in that jurisdiction to help you create the plan. Therefore, if a lawyer for a client who has property in Florida is not a Florida resident, they should get a Florida lawyer to help them.

- A second key strategy in this area is to read estate planning documents carefully— make sure you understand what they say and make sure the client understands them as well. Sometimes you have to sit down with the client and explain to them in laypeople's terms how the documents work, make sure they understand what you are saying, and then ask them if that is what they want to have happen.

Brian V. McAvoy, a partner at Harter Secrest & Emery LLP, serves individuals and businesses throughout southwest Florida. Mr. McAvoy's practice areas include estate planning, estate and trust administration, probate litigation, general business, and real estate law. He is a board-certified specialist in estate planning and probate law as recognized by the Florida Bar. Mr. McAvoy is also the partner in charge of the firm's office in Naples, Florida.

Mr. McAvoy is a member of the board of directors at the David Lawrence Center and of the Professional Advisors Council of The Community Foundation of Collier County. He is member and past president of Kiwanis Club of Naples and member of the Estate Planning Council of Naples.

Mr. McAvoy was selected by his peers for inclusion in The Best Lawyers in America *in the field of Trust and Estates and for inclusion in* Super Lawyers, *2009, for Estate Planning & Probate and Closely Held Business.*

Mr. McAvoy received his J.D., cum laude, from State University of New York at Buffalo and his B.A. from Hamilton College.

89

APPENDICES

Appendix A: Durable Power of Attorney   92

Appendix B: Irrevocable Trust Used to Own and Hold
Life Insurance   100

Appendix C: Will with Testamentary Trust   116

Appendix D: Confidential Estate Planning Questionnaire   124

Appendix E: Objectives Worksheet   139

Appendix F: Legacy Management Program   141

APPENDIX A

DURABLE POWER OF ATTORNEY

KNOW ALL MEN BY THESE PRESENTS, that I, _____, the Grantor, of _____, do hereby make, constitute and appoint my _____, _____, of _____, to serve as my true and lawful Attorney-in-Fact, and if he/she is deceased, incapable or declines in writing to act as Attorney-in-Fact, Grantor appoints _____, of _____, both of whom are collectively referred to herein as my "attorney-in-fact," to exercise the powers and discretions set forth below either (1) alone and without the approval or consent of any other attorney-in-fact named herein, or (2) jointly with any other attorney-in-fact named herein. Incapability shall be conclusively established by a letter of opinion from such Attorney-in-Fact's physician.

This Durable Power of Attorney does make the above-named my true and lawful attorney to make, execute, sign, endorse or deliver any and all documents in Grantor's name or on behalf of Grantor, including specifically power to convey and mortgage Grantor's real and personal property and all of Grantor's interest in such property, without reservation or limitation, it being Grantor's intention to hereby comply with and extend **all of the authority contained in Florida Statutes Section 709.08** and any amendments thereof and any successor statutory provision(s) thereto. This Durable Power of Attorney applies to any interest in property now or hereafter owned, held or acquired by Grantor, including, without limitation: Grantor's interest in real property, including homestead real property; all personal property, tangible or intangible; all property held in any type of joint tenancy, including a tenancy in common, joint tenancy with right of survivorship or a tenancy by the entirety; all property over which Grantor holds a general, limited or special power of appointment; choses in action; and other contractual or statutory rights or elections, including, but not limited to, any rights or elections in any probate or similar proceeding to which Grantor is or may become entitled.

My attorney(s) appointed hereunder are hereby given and granted full power and authority to do and perform all and every act and thing whatsoever requisite and necessary to be done in and about the premises as

APPENDICES

fully, to all intents and purposes, as Grantor might or could do if personally present, hereby ratifying and confirming all that such attorney(s) shall lawfully do or cause to be done by virtue hereof, including but not limited to the following:

A.   To arrange for and consent to medical, therapeutical and surgical procedures for Grantor, including the administration of **or the withholding of** drugs, nutrition and hydration; to make all health care decisions on behalf of Grantor including but not limited to those set forth in Chapter 765 Florida Statutes; to act generally and fully as **HEALTH CARE SURROGATE** for Grantor in all matters pertaining to the care and well-being of Grantor; to carry out and implement any and all directions that Grantor may have given by a "Living Will". No proceeding initiated in any court shall affect any authority of the attorney-in-fact to make health care decisions for Grantor, including but not limited to those defined in Chapter 765 Florida Statutes, unless otherwise ordered by a court of competent jurisdiction. Notwithstanding the provision of this paragraph, should there be a conflict with the terms or named parties of my living will, then and in that event the terms of the living will shall override the terms of this paragraph.

B.   To have access to any and all of my medical records, including any of my records to Medicare or Medicaid, (to complete, sign and deliver any Written Authorization Form required by any provider and have authority to authorize release of such information to appropriate persons), including but not limited to, any documents protected by patient-physician privilege, attorney-client privilege, or the Health Insurance Portability and Accountability Act of 1996 ("HIPAA").

C.   To take care of, contract for, make arrangements for and make financial commitments for, on my behalf, my medical care and attention, including, without limiting the foregoing, to engage doctors and nurses and health care aides, to provide hospitalization, to consent to operations, to call ambulances and to provide any required consents to medication and any other medical procedures; provided, however, if at any time a Health Care Surrogate is acting on my behalf, my attorney-in-fact shall cooperate with, follow the directive of, and provide any necessary financial assistance, using my property, to such Health Care Surrogate. In addition to the other powers granted by this document, my attorney-in-fact shall have the power and authority to serve as my personal representative for all purposes of the Health Insurance Portability and Accountability Act of 1996, (Pub. L. 104-191), 45 CFR Section 160 through 164. It is my intent, however, that the expressions of this paragraph and any other authority granted in this instrument shall not be used or applied in a manner that will disqualify me from receiving any governmental subsidies to which I may be entitled.

D. To create, fund, amend or modify an Irrevocable Income Trust and/or a Special Needs Trust as may, in the sole discretion of my attorney-in-fact, be necessary and for my best interest in accordance with the provisions of the Omnibus Budget Reconciliation Act of 1993 as passed by U.S. Congress or any amendments thereto, or any other Trust to qualify Grantor for Medicaid benefits.

E. To apply for public benefits on my behalf with any federal, state or local agency, without restriction, and to receive and apply such benefits on my behalf; to maximize my entitlement to federal and state medical, welfare, housing and other programs, by all legitimate and proper means within the sound and trusted discretion of my attorney-in-fact. The authority herein granted shall include but not be limited to converting my assets into assets that do not disqualify me from receiving such benefits or divesting me of such assets.

F. To deal with all retirement plans of which I am a member including individual retirement accounts, rollovers, and voluntary contribution; to direct any pension fund, insurance, or annuity company, the United States Social Security Administration, or any other party making payments to me to make such payments directly to a financial institution for direct deposit into my account.

G. To manage any and all property, real or personal, tangible or intangible, wherever situated; to sell, convey, assign, mortgage, encumber or otherwise transfer the same; to lease same; to foreclose mortgages or enforce any other rights with respect to the same; to take title to the same in my name; and to execute, acknowledge and deliver deeds, bills of sale, mortgages, releases, satisfactions and any other instruments relating to the same which such attorney, in the exercise of absolute discretion, shall deem appropriate.

APPENDICES

H.   To execute a deed or mortgage of homestead realty; to join in the conveyance or mortgage of homestead realty; including the power to convey, mortgage, join and deal in any way with any subsequently obtained homestead property.

I.   To do business with banks and brokers, and particularly to endorse all checks and drafts made payable to my order and collect the proceeds; to sign in my name checks on all accounts standing in my name; to withdraw funds from said accounts; to open accounts in my name or in the name of such attorney, as my attorney-in-fact.

J.   To borrow money from any lender, personal or corporate, and to extend or renew any existing indebtedness of mine.

K.   To compromise, contest, prosecute or abandon claims in favor of or against me.

L.   To have access at any time or times to any safe deposit box to which I have access, or any safe deposit box rented by me, wheresoever located, and to remove all or any part of the contents thereof, and to surrender or relinquish said safe deposit box; and any institution in which any such safe deposit box may be located shall not incur any liability to me or my estate as a result of permitting my attorney-in-fact to exercise this power.

M.   To transfer, convert, endorse, sell, assign, set over and deliver any and all shares of stock, bonds (including but not limited to U.S. Treasury bonds and U.S. Savings bonds), debentures, notes, subscription warrants, stock purchase warrants, evidences of indebtedness, or other securities now or hereafter standing in my name or owned by me and to make, execute and deliver any and all written instruments of assignment and transfer necessary or proper to effectuate the authority hereby conferred.

N.   To ask, demand, sue for, collect and receive all sums of money, dividends, interest, payments on account of debts and legacies and all property now due or which may hereafter become due and owning to me, and give good and valid receipts and discharges for such payment; to buy and sell securities of all kinds in my name and for my account and at such

95

INSIDE THE MINDS

prices as such attorney, in the exercise of absolute discretion, shall deem appropriate.

O.   To vote any corporate securities for any purpose; to exercise or sell any subscription or conversion rights; to consent to and join in or oppose any voting trusts, reorganizations, consolidations, mergers, foreclosures and liquidations and in connection therewith to deposit securities and accept and hold other securities or property received therefor.

P.   To conduct or participate in any lawful business of whatever nature for me and in my name; to execute partnership agreements and amendments thereto; to incorporate, reorganize, merge, consolidate, recapitalize, sell, liquidate, or dissolve any business; to elect or employ officers, directors and agents; to carry out the provision of any agreement for the sale of any business interest or the stock therein; and to exercise stock options.

Q.   To apply for a Certificate of Title upon, and endorse and transfer title thereto, for any automobile, truck, pickup, van, motorcycle or other motor vehicle, boat, trailer, or mobile home, and to represent in such transfer assignment that the title to said motor vehicle, boat, trailer or mobile home is free and clear of all liens and encumbrances except those specifically set forth in such transfer assignment.

R.   To prepare, sign and file joint or separate income tax returns or declarations of estimated tax for any year or years; to prepare, sign and file gift tax returns with respect to gifts made by me for any year or years; to consent to any gift and to utilize any gift-splitting provisions or other tax election, and to prepare, sign, and file any claims for refund of any tax; and to represent me in all income tax matters before any office of the Internal Revenue Service, within the limitations of the applicable Revenue Rulings and Procedures; to file any state, county or municipal tax returns of any kind or nature and to negotiate with any and all taxing authorities, and to compromise any disputes which may arise with any such agency.

S.   To create an inter vivos trust on my behalf and to fund such inter vivos trust or to fund a previously established inter vivos trust so long as such trust does not conflict with any existing testamentary plan of mine.

96

APPENDICES

T.   To transfer assets to the then acting Trustee of any Declaration of Trust executed by me with myself as Settlor (or Grantor).

U.   To establish a custodian or other type of investment account with any bank, trust company, investment broker, or other securities dealer.

V.   To retain such accountants, attorneys, social workers, consultants, clerks, employees, workmen, or other persons as my agent shall deem appropriate in connection with the management of my property and affairs and to make payments from my assets for the charges of such person so employed.

W.   To make such payments and expenditures as such attorney shall, in the exercise of absolute discretion, determine to be necessary in connection with any of the foregoing matters or with the administration of my affairs.

X.   My attorney-in-fact shall be entitled to reimbursement for all reasonable expenses incurred as a result of carrying out any provision of this Durable Power of Attorney, and shall be released from any and all liability for good faith efforts.

Y.   This Durable Power of Attorney is non-delegable except for the following as provided in F.S. 709.08(7)(a) 1&2:

1. The authority to execute stock powers or similar documents on my behalf and delegate to a transfer agent or similar person the authority to transfer and register any stocks, bonds, or other securities either into or out of my name.
2. The authority to convey or mortgage homestead property. If I am married, the attorney-in-fact may not mortgage or convey homestead property without joinder of my spouse or my spouse's legal guardian. Joinder by my spouse may be accomplished by the exercise of authority in a durable power of attorney executed by the joining spouse, and either spouse may appoint the other as the attorney-in-fact.

Z.   Banking institutions, savings and loan institutions and stock brokerage firms and stock transfer agents, as well as all other third persons, are authorized to rely on the provisions of this Durable Power of Attorney and are exonerated from any loss, claim or liability in relying on said instrument and its provisions. Parties dealing with my attorney-in-fact named herein are not required to investigate or determine such attorney-in-fact's authority, or the validity, or the advisability of the transactions, to see to the proper exercise of powers, or to follow the disposition of monies and/or property delivered to my attorney-in-fact hereunder. A third party who acts in good faith upon any representation, direction, decision, or act of the attorney-in-fact is not liable to the principal or the principal's estate, beneficiaries, or joint owners for those acts. My attorney-in-fact shall execute any affidavit as may be required by a third party to verify my attorney-in-fact's authority to act under this document.

AA. **To exercise each and all of these powers in any state, country or legal jurisdiction as fully as though this instrument had been executed pursuant to the laws thereof.**

BB. My attorney-in-fact may exercise the authority granted under this durable power of attorney until I die, revoke the power, or am adjudicated totally or partially incapacitated by the court of competent jurisdiction, unless the court determines that certain authority granted by the durable power of attorney is to remain exercisable by my attorney-in-fact. (FS §709.08(3)(b))

By this instrument I hereby revoke any power of attorney, durable or otherwise, that I may have recorded prior to the date of this Durable Power of Attorney.

IN WITNESS WHEREOF, Grantor has executed and sealed this instrument this _____day of _____, ____.

Sealed and delivered in the presence of:

_____   _____(Seal)
                                        _____, Grantor

_____

STATE OF FLORIDA
COUNTY OF PINELLAS

APPENDICES

The foregoing instrument was acknowledged before me this _____day of _____, _____, by _____, who is personally known to me, or who produced a driver's license as identification, and witnessed by _____, who is personally known to me, or who produced a driver's license as identification, and _____, who is personally known to me, or who produced a driver's license as identification.

_____(Seal)Notary Public
My Commission Expires:

Courtesy of Elwood Hogan Jr., McFarland, Gould, Lyons, Sullivan & Hogan PA

Appendix B

IRREVOCABLE TRUST USED TO OWN AND HOLD LIFE INSURANCE

TRUST AGREEMENT

THIS TRUST AGREEMENT dated _____, ____, between _____, of _____ County, Florida, hereinafter referred to as "Grantor", and _____, hereinafter referred to as "Trustee". In the event _____. is unable, unwilling or disqualified to serve, then _____ shall serve as successor Trustee. In the event _____ is unable, unwilling or disqualified to serve, then _____ shall serve as second successor Trustee.

WHEREAS, the Grantor desires to create a trust to receive certain assets which may be gifted by the Grantor to the Trustee to be held hereunder;

WHEREAS, the Grantor has, upon the establishment of this trust, gifted to the Trustee the assets described in Exhibit "A" attached hereto and made a part hereof (such original assets so listed) together with any additional monies, securities and other assets that the Trustee may hereafter at any time hold or acquire from Grantor or any person or entity and the proceeds and the reinvestments thereof are hereby collectively called the "Trust Estate";

WHEREAS, the Grantor hereby declares this trust to be irrevocable, expressly waiving the right to alter, amend or revoke this trust, and hereby irrevocably assign, transfer and set over to the Trustee all of the rights and interests they have in and to the trust estate, and the Trustee has agreed to hold the trust estate as hereinafter set forth;

WHEREAS, to carry out the principal purpose of this trust, the Trustee may utilize such assets to purchase life insurance policies upon the life of the Grantor for the benefit of the Grantor's beneficiaries as herein provided, but the Grantor shall not possess any rights, powers, options, title, claims or other benefits in and to such policies;

APPENDICES

NOW, THEREFORE, in consideration of the promises and mutual covenants herein contained, the Grantor and the Trustee hereby agree that the Trustee is vested with all right, title and interest in and to the trust estate, and the Trustee is authorized and empowered to exercise, as the fiduciary owner of the trust estate, all of the options, benefits, rights and privileges relating to the assets constituting the trust estate and the proceeds and reinvestments thereof, including the fiduciary power to amend this trust as might be necessary to preserve Grantor's desired tax consequence and treatment to comply with the rules and regulations of the Internal Revenue Service, it being Grantor's specific intent that all gift contributions to this trust shall qualify as a present interest gift, and the Trustee further agrees to hold, invest, reinvest and otherwise deal with the trust estate as hereinafter provided.

ARTICLE I
Disposition of Trust Estate during Grantor's Lifetime

During the time that the Grantor shall be living, the Trustee may pay from the income and principal of the trust estate any premiums or assessments on any policy of life insurance held by the Trustee for the benefit of the trust estate. The Trustee shall hold the trust property as a separate trust estate and shall divide such property into such number of shares as hereinafter provided in this trust agreement and subject to the terms and conditions as set forth herein for the benefit of the Grantor's named primary beneficiaries: _____ .

ARTICLE II
Dealings with the Grantor's Estate

The Trustee is hereby authorized, in the absolute discretion of the Trustee, without regard to whether it shall be serving as a personal representative of the Grantor's estate to purchase on behalf of the trust estate any property, real, personal or mixed, tangible or intangible, and wherever situated, belonging to the estate of Grantor, or, to make loans or advancements, secured or unsecured, to the personal representative of the estate of Grantor. Any such purchases, loans or advancements shall be made upon such terms and conditions as the Trustee shall deem in its sole discretion appropriate, and the Trustee shall not be liable for any loss to the trust estate by reason of acting in accordance with this ARTICLE II, except for the Trustee's malfeasance or gross negligence. The Trustee shall not, in any manner, be required to purchase any of such assets from Grantor's estate or, to make any such loans or advancements to Grantor's estate.

ARTICLE III
Residuary Trust Estate and Disposition of Residuary Trust Estate

(A) Upon the death of the Grantor, the Trustee shall deal with the Residuary Trust Estate as hereafter provided.

(B) Such assets of the Residuary Trust Estate shall be divided into shares necessary to effectuate the following distribution:

_____	___ shares
_____	___ shares
_____	___ shares

Upon the death of a beneficiary for whom a share of trust property is being held in trust hereunder, such deceased beneficiary's share shall be paid pro-rata to the surviving beneficiaries named hereunder. If there are no surviving beneficiaries hereunder, then such trust property shall be distributed to the _____ to perpetuate the _____ SCHOLARSHIP FUND.

ARTICLE IV
Discretionary Powers With Respect to Distributions of Income or Principal

(A) This Article shall apply to each share created under ARTICLE III of this Agreement. For purposes of this Article, the term "Beneficiary" shall mean at any time, with relation to each such trust, the person to whom at that time, under such provisions, all or any part of the current net income from such trust could properly be paid in the absence of the exercise of the discretionary powers conferred on the Trustee by the provisions of this Article.

APPENDICES

(B) The Trustee is hereby authorized, in the case of each such trust, from time to time and in the absolute discretion of the Trustee:

(1) to pay to the Beneficiary so much of the principal of such trust as the Trustee shall deem necessary or advisable (a) for the maintenance and welfare of the Beneficiary, (b) for accidents, illness or other emergencies (of a similar or a different nature) affecting the Beneficiary, or (c) for any other purpose which the Trustee shall deem to be worthwhile and in the best interests of the Beneficiary; and

(2) to withhold from the Beneficiary all or any part of the income which could properly be paid to the Beneficiary and to accumulate it and add it to the principal of such trust.

(3) if at any time the Trustee shall be of the opinion that continuance of such trust is neither necessary nor desirable in the interest of the Beneficiary, to terminate such trust by distributing the entire principal thereof to the Beneficiary without further accountability therefore to anyone.

(C) The powers granted by the foregoing provisions of this Article shall be exercised in such manner as the Trustee shall believe will serve the best interests of the Beneficiary, rather than for remainder or other successor interests. In connection with the exercise of such powers, the Trustee shall be justified in relying conclusively, without investigation, on any information furnished to it by the Beneficiary.

(D) Notwithstanding any provision hereof to the contrary, during the life of the Grantor, each of Grantor's beneficiaries as set forth hereinabove, shall, in each fiscal year of this trust, have an absolute or unrestricted right or power to withdraw from this trust an amount either in cash or in kind up to the value of the total additions (including the cash value of any life insurance policies and the gift tax value of any premiums paid by any person or entity on policies on the life of the Grantor which are deemed to be indirect transfers by the Grantor to the trust) made to this trust during each fiscal year multiplied by the designated share of such beneficiary stated above. The power of withdrawal of a beneficiary is non-cumulative, and such right of withdrawal by a beneficiary shall be exercised by such beneficiary notifying the Trustee in writing to that effect. The Trustee shall

103

promptly thereafter make any requested distribution to the beneficiary. After receipt by the Trustee of any addition to the trust estate from any person or entity, the Trustee shall give written notice to each beneficiary who shall have the right of withdrawal as provided in this Subparagraph (D) of each such beneficiary's right of withdrawal, and such beneficiary shall have thirty (30) days from receipt of such written notice in order to deliver to the Trustee the written withdrawal request of such beneficiary. Such written notice shall be given by the Trustee to a beneficiary shall be in a form similar to Exhibit "B". If such beneficiary does not properly deliver such written withdrawal request within such time period, the withdrawal rights of that beneficiary with respect to that addition shall lapse. Upon the death of a beneficiary, the right of withdrawal of such beneficiary shall cease as to that deceased beneficiary. In no event shall the total amount withdrawable by a beneficiary by reason of an addition or additions to his or her lifetime separate trust in any one calendar year exceed the gift tax annual exclusion. This annual limit on withdrawals shall apply for each beneficiary, and the annual exclusion shall not limit the cumulative amount of annual withdrawals for all beneficiaries. The gift tax annual exclusion shall be as provided under Section 2503(b) of the Internal Revenue Code (currently $_____ per beneficiary) or any other corresponding provisions of any subsequent federal tax laws in effect in the calendar year of withdrawal.

ARTICLE V
Provisions for Limitation of
Duration and Ultimate Remainder of Trusts

Notwithstanding any provision of this Agreement to the contrary, no trust or interest created herein shall continue for the later of: (i) _____ (__) years after the creation of such trust or interest; or (ii) _____ (__) years after the death of the last of all the beneficiaries hereunder who are living at the death of the Grantors. Each trust so terminated shall be distributed, in equal shares, free of trust to the beneficiary or beneficiaries then entitled to the income from such trust.

If upon the death of the Grantors, the whole or part of the trust estate, or, upon the termination of any trust created under this agreement the whole or part of the principal of such trust, shall not be effectively disposed of by or pursuant to the provisions elsewhere in this agreement contained, the Grantors direct that the property constituting such whole or part shall thereupon be distributed to the Grantors' heirs as determined as of Grantors' deaths.

ARTICLE VI
Miscellaneous Powers of Trustee

The Trustee or Successor Trustee shall have full power:

A. To make any or all portions of the payments or distributions hereinabove provided, including final distribution, in any one or more of the following manners:

(1) Directly to any beneficiary entitled thereto;
(2) To the legal guardian or conservator of such beneficiary;
(3) To a relative of such beneficiary to be expended by such relative for the benefit of such beneficiary;
(4) By said Trustee expending the same for the benefit of such beneficiary; and the decision of the Trustee in each case shall be final and binding upon all beneficiaries hereunder.

B. To invest and reinvest the Trust Estate or any part thereof in any property, real or personal, including, without limitation, common and preferred stock and any securities of any nature as Trustee shall deem wise, without being limited to investments authorized by law for trust funds.

C. To cause any security or other property which may at any time constitute a portion of the Trust Estate, to be issued, held or registered in said Trustee's own name or in the name of a nominee or in such form that title will pass by delivery.

D. In respect to any securities, to vote upon any proposition or election at any meeting and to grant proxies, discretionary or otherwise, and to vote at any such meeting.

E. To determine what is "income" and what is "principal" hereunder, in said Trustee's sole discretion, without regard to any statute or rule of law.

INSIDE THE MINDS

F. To mortgage, sell or pledge any property, real or personal, at any time constituting any portion or portions of the Trust Estate or the entire Trust Estate upon such terms and conditions as the Trustee shall deem wise.

G. To retain any assets distributed to Trustee by Grantor's Personal Representative, in kind, without regard to any rule of prudent trust management.

H. To employ legal counsel, accountants, investment advisors, brokers or other agents or employees have to pay to them reasonable compensation.

I. To exercise any and all powers and discretions given to a Trustee under the Florida Trust Administration Law and the other laws of the State of Florida not inconsistent with the provisions hereof, and to do all other acts necessary for the proper and advantageous management, investment and distribution of the Trust Estate. Compliance with F.S. 738.12 and F.S. 738.13 is waived.

ARTICLE VII
Other Provisions Concerning Trustee

(A) The trustee serving hereunder shall receive such compensation, if any, as shall have been provided for in a written agreement between such Trustee and the Grantors or the other person or persons who shall have appointed such trustee as hereinafter provided, or, in the absence of any such agreement, as shall be reasonable under the laws of the State of Florida, or, for a corporate trustee, such compensation as shall be stated on such corporate trustee's schedule of fees in effect at the time that such services are rendered.

(B) If, at any time, a trust hereunder has a market value, as determined by the Trustee, of $50,000.00 or less, the Trustee, in its sole discretion, may terminate this trust and distribute the property therein proportionately to the persons then entitled to receive or have the benefit of the income therefrom.

(C) To the full extent legally possible, the Trustee named hereunder is hereby released from any obligation in any jurisdiction, to furnish any bond

106

APPENDICES

or other security, to file any inventory, to render any annual or other periodic accountings, or to obtain the approval of any court before applying, distributing, selling or otherwise dealing with any property.

(D) The trustee may resign by instrument signed and acknowledged by it and delivered to its successor trustee, or, if none, to the then adult income beneficiaries of the trust provided hereunder; provided, however, that if a trustee is resigning, such resignation shall not be effective until another individual or corporation shall have been appointed as a successor trustee and shall have accepted the appointment.

(E)   The interest of a beneficiary in the principal or income of this trust shall not be subject to claims of the beneficiary's creditors, or others, or liable to attachment, execution or other process of law, and the beneficiary shall have no right to encumber, hypothecate or alienate any interest in this trust in any manner. The Trustee may, however, deposit in any bank, designated in writing by the beneficiary to the beneficiary's credit, any income or principal payable to the beneficiary.

ARTICLE VIII
Insurance

(A) The Grantor expressly relinquishes and vests in the Trustee all rights, options and privileges in and to any and all insurance policies under which this trust agreement is designated as the beneficiary. Such rights, options and privileges shall include, without limitation, the right to borrow or assign such policy, the right to change the beneficiary thereunder, the right to convert such policies into such other forms of insurance as the Trustee shall determine and the right to receive all payments of any kind under such policies. The Trustee shall not be responsible for the payment of the premium on such insurance policies, but the Trustee may make such payment if the Trustee determines, in his sole discretion, to do so. The Trustee shall incur no liability for any action taken by the Trustee or for the Trustee's omission to take any action and exercise in good faith of the rights and powers hereinabove conferred upon the Trustee. The Grantor shall perform all acts and make, execute and deliver any instruments necessary in order to give effect to the designation of this trust agreement as the beneficiary of such life insurance policies, or, to transfer the ownership of

107

INSIDE THE MINDS

any life insurance policies to the trustee in such fiduciary capacity. The Trustee shall receive the proceeds of any insurance policies payable to this trust agreement and to add such proceeds to the trust estate hereunder.

(B) After the death of the Grantor, the Trustee shall file a claim for and shall receive the proceeds of the policies then becoming payable to the Trustee of this trust agreement. The Trustee shall have the power to execute and deliver receipts and other instruments and to take such action as is appropriate to the collection of such proceeds. In the event the payment of any proceeds on such policy or policies is contested, however, the Trustee shall be under no obligation to institute legal action for the collection thereof unless and until it has been indemnified to its satisfaction against any loss, liability or expense, including attorneys' fees. The Trustee may reimburse itself from the trust estate for any advances made by it for the collection of such proceeds. It is the intent of the Grantor and the Trustee that only the net proceeds of such insurance policies payable to the Trustee of this trust agreement shall be collected hereunder, and accordingly, all loans, advances and other charges against any such policies shall be paid from the proceeds thereof, and only the remaining proceeds shall be claimed and collected by the Trustee hereunder.

(C) No insurance company issuing any policy of insurance payable to the Trustee of this trust agreement shall be responsible for the application or disposition of the proceeds of such policy by the Trustee. Payment to and receipt by the Trustee of such proceeds shall be a full discharge of the liability of such insurance company under such policy.

ARTICLE IX
Revocation or Amendment

Any trust hereby created shall be irrevocable, and the Grantor expressly waives all rights and powers, whether along or in conjunction with others, and regardless of when or from what source they may heretofore or hereafter have acquired such rights or powers, to alter, amend, revoke or terminate the trust or any of the terms of this trust agreement in whole or in part. The Grantors hereby relinquish absolutely and forever all their possession or enjoyment of or right to the principal and income from the

APPENDICES

trust estate, and all of the Grantors' rights and powers, whether alone or in conjunction with others, to designate the persons or entities who shall possess and enjoy the trust estate or the income therefrom.

ARTICLE X
Governing Law

The trusts created hereby shall be Florida trusts and shall be administered in accordance with the laws of that State and the validity and effect of the provisions hereof shall be determined in accordance with those laws.

ARTICLE XI
Provisions Regarding Right to
Receive Income or Principal

Except as otherwise provided herein, the right of any person to receive any amount, whether of income or of principal, pursuant to any of the provisions of this agreement, shall not, in any manner, be anticipated, alienated, assigned or encumbered and shall not be subject to any legal process, bankruptcy, insolvency proceeding or to interference or control by creditors or others.

ARTICLE XII
Definitions

(A) Whenever, on the occurrence of any event, any property shall be required by any of the provisions of this agreement to be distributed to the Distributees of an individual, such property shall be distributed to the persons who would be entitled thereto, and in the shares to which such persons would be entitled, under the laws of the State of Florida then in effect, if such individual had died immediately after the occurrence of such event, intestate and domiciled in that State, and such property had constituted his entire net distributable estate.

(B) Wherever used in this agreement, except where the context shall clearly require otherwise:

    (1) the term "property" shall include real, personal and mixed property, tangible or intangible, of any kind and wherever

109

located, including securities and interests in any so-called common trust funds;

(2) the term "securities" shall include bonds, mortgages, notes, obligations, warrants and stocks of any class, and such other evidences of indebtedness and certificates of interest as are usually referred to by the term "securities";

(3) the term "trustee" shall mean at any time with relation to any trust hereunder the trustee or trustees of that trust then in office;

(4) words in either the masculine or the feminine form shall be deemed to include or relate to both males and females and, where appropriate, corporations or other entities;

(5) words either in the singular or the plural number shall be deemed to include both the singular and the plural numbers;

(6) for purposes of convenience, this trust shall be known as the "Irrevocable Life Insurance Trust of Jean Lester Bennett".

IN WITNESS WHEREOF, the Grantor has signed this agreement, this _____ day of _____, ____.

WITNESSES:

_____   _____(Seal)

_____, Grantor

STATE OF FLORIDA
COUNTY OF _____

We, _____, _____ and _____, respectively, whose names are signed to the attached or foregoing instrument, being first duly sworn, do hereby declare to the undersigned officer that the Grantor signed the instrument as her Trust Agreement and that she signed voluntarily and that each of the witnesses, in the presence of the Grantor, at her request, and in the presence of each other, signed the instrument as a witness, and that to the best of the knowledge of each witness, the Grantor was at that time 18 or more years of age, of sound mind and under no constraint or undue influence.

Grantor

Witness

Witness

SUBSCRIBED AND ACKNOWLEDGED before me by
_____, the Grantor, and subscribed and
sworn to before me by   and   the
Witnesses, all personally known to me, this   day of _____,
_____.

Notary Public
My commission expires:

TRUSTEE ACCEPTANCE

_____ hereby accepts the fiduciary duties, powers and authorities in him/her vested by the Irrevocable Trust of _____ dated _____, _____.

_____, Trustee

STATE OF FLORIDA
COUNTY OF _____

The foregoing instrument was acknowledged before me this   day of _____, _____, by _____, who is personally known to me (or who has produced _____ as identification).

Notary Public
My commission expires:

APPENDICES

EXHIBIT "A"

To the Irrevocable Trust of
_____ dated _____

Cash Payment $_____

EXHIBIT "B"

To the Irrevocable Trust of

_____ dated _____

Re: Notice of Annual Contribution to the Irrevocable Trust
        of _____ dated _____

Dear Beneficiary:

Please be advised that on the _____ day of _____, _____, we have received the annual gift for the above referenced trust in the amount of $_____. These funds have been deposited to the trust's account and you are hereby noticed that should you desire to withdraw same for your own benefit you may do so within thirty (30) days of your receipt hereof by so notifying the Trustee, _____, at _____, _____, FL _____. Your election to withdraw your pro-rata share of the above specified gift should be made in writing and posted by certified or registered mail.

Your withdrawal right is noncumulative and to the extent you do not exercise it, will lapse thirty (30) days of your receipt of this notification.

Yours sincerely,

_____, Trustee

APPENDICES

ACKNOWLEDGMENT OF NOTICE

I acknowledge receipt of this Notification of Demand Right.

Dated:

(Beneficiary's name)

Courtesy of Elwood Hogan Jr., McFarland, Gould, Lyons, Sullivan & Hogan PA

Appendix C

WILL WITH TESTAMENTARY TRUST

LAST WILL AND TESTAMENT
OF

_____

I, _____, a resident of the State of Florida, being of sound and disposing mind and memory, do hereby make, publish and declare this to be my Last Will and Testament, hereby revoking and annulling all other Wills and Codicils by me heretofore made.

I.

I hereby direct that all of my just debts and funeral expenses be paid as soon after my death as practicable.

II.

I give and devise such of my tangible personal property to those persons designated in a separate writing in existence at the time of my death which is signed by me and which describes the items and devisees with reasonable certainty, as permitted by Chapter 732.515, Florida Statutes 1995, or any effective revision thereof. If no such list is found within sixty (60) days after the date of my death, it shall be conclusively presumed that no such valid list exists.

III.
(SPECIFIC DEVISE)

IV.
(SPECIFIC DEVISE)

V.
(SPECIFIC DEVISE)

I give and devise _____, in equal share to _____, or the survivor of them. Such division

APPENDICES

shall be handled by my Personal Representative so that this collection is divided in equal dollar value.

VI.

I give and devise my _____, if owned by me at the time of my death, to my _____, _____, if surviving me. My Personal Representative shall not release this bequest to _____ until ___ has satisfactorily completed his certification of LARAN or GPS and a Coast Guard approved boating course.

VII.

I give and devise to my _____, _____, the sum of _____ DOLLARS ($_____). It being my concern that my _____ have sufficient funds for his personal care in his responsibilities and duties as guardian of my _____, _____. In the event my _____, _____, has reached the age of majority, this bequest shall remain in favor of my _____. In the event my father predeceases me this bequest shall lapse and become a part of my residuary estate.

VIII.

All the rest, residue and remainder of my estate, whether real property, personal property or mixed, of whatever nature or kind and wheresoever situated of which I may die seized and possessed, or which I may own or have an interest in at the time of my death, I give and devise to _____, as Trustee, **IN TRUST**, however, for my children, _____ **and** _____, per stirpes. If _____ cannot serve as Trustee, then and in that event _____ shall serve as Trustee.

I hereby instruct my Trustee to first transfer the sum of $_____ from life insurance proceeds, of which my estate is the beneficiary, into the cash operational banking account of _____, if such business is owned by me at the time of my death.

I hereby instruct my Trustee that my commercial real estate, improvements thereon, and all of my stock ownership in _____ and _____ owned by me at the time of my death, shall remain an asset of this trust, notwithstanding the general provisions contained hereafter in this instrument, until my _____, _____, attains the age of _____ (__) years, at which time said portion of my Trust shall terminate and my Trustee shall distribute same in equal shares to my children, _____ and _____, per stirpes.

All other assets that I leave in Trust at the time of my death, I instruct my Trustee to divide into two equal trust shares, one for the benefit of each of my children named herein, and said Trustee shall pay so much of the income thereof and so much of the principal, excepting the commercial property, as may be necessary, in the sole discretion of the Trustee, for the health, maintenance, and education of my children.

Upon each of my children reaching the age of thirty-five (35) years, the Trustee shall distribute one-third of such child's trust principal, together with all accumulated income, if any.

Upon each of my children reaching the age of forty-five (45) years, the Trustee shall distribute one-half of such child's trust principal, together with all accumulated income, if any.

Upon each child reaching the age of fifty-five (55) years, the Trustee shall distribute the balance of such child's trust principal, and all accumulated income, if any.

If either of my children shall predecease me or die during the administration of his trust, such deceased child's trust or balance thereof shall pass, per stirpes and be administered by my Trustee under the same trust terms as hereinabove set forth.

In the event one of my said children shall die without issue, then such child's share shall lapse and pass to the surviving child.

PROVIDED, HOWEVER, if a grandchild becomes an immediate receiving beneficiary and has not attained the age of thirty-five (35) years,

APPENDICES

such grandchild's share shall continue in trust with all income being paid to or for the benefit of such grandchild in the Trustee's sole discretion, until he or she reaches the age of thirty-five (35) years, at which time that grandchild's trust shall terminate with the Trustee paying or distributing the remaining trust Res and all accumulated income, if any, to said grandchild.

IX.

Said Trustee shall have full power:

1. To make any or all portions of the payments or distributions hereinabove provided, including final distribution, in any one or more of the following manners:

    (a) To the legal guardian or conservator of such beneficiary;
    (b) To a relative of a beneficiary to be expended by such relative for the benefit of the beneficiary;
    (c) By the Trustee expending, including the power and authority to sell and convey, for the benefit of a beneficiary; and the decision of the Trustee in each case shall be final and binding upon all beneficiaries hereunder.

2. To invest and reinvest the trust estate or any part thereof in any property, real or personal, including without limitation, common and preferred stock and any securities of any nature as Trustee shall deem wise, without being limited to investments authorized by law for trust funds.

3. To cause any security or other property which may at any time constitute a portion of the trust estate to be issued, held or registered in said Trustee's own names or in the name of a nominee or in such form that title will pass by delivery.

4. In respect to any securities, to vote upon any proposition or election at any meeting and to grant proxies, discretionary or otherwise, and to vote at any such meeting.

5. To determine what is "income" and what is "principal" hereunder, in said Trustee's sole discretion, without regard to any statute or rule of law.

6. I direct that Florida Statutes 737 shall not apply and I specifically exempt the terms of this trust from said statute.

7. To possess full power and authority to hold, manage, mortgage, sell and convey any real property becoming a part of the above stated Trust.

X.

The portions of my estate that are held in Trust following my death, whether referring to my son or grandchildren, shall be subject to the instructions and limitations as follows:

Such portion of Trust assets shall not be a resource to the beneficiary. It shall not be available to him or her except in the Trustee's discretion, and then only to the extent that other resources are not available to provide for the beneficiary's supplemental care needs. The Trustee owes no duty to the Beneficiary. Further, this is a spendthrift trust. None of the principal or income of the trust estate nor any interest in the trust may be anticipated, assigned, encumbered, or be made subject to any creditors' claims, or to any legal process. No part of the trust estate shall be subject to the claims of voluntary or involuntary creditors of the beneficiary, including any agency of the State of Florida, or any other state, or of the United States. No part of the principal or income of the trust estate shall be payable to the beneficiary's creditors during the beneficiary's life or following the beneficiary's death.

Under no circumstances can the beneficiary nor any creditor compel a distribution from the trust for any purpose. The Trustee's discretion in making non-support disbursement as provided for in this instrument is final as to all interested parties, including the state or any governmental agency or agencies, even if the Trustee elects to make no disbursements at all. Further, the Trustee may be arbitrary and unreasonable. The Trustee's sole and independent judgment, rather than the determination of any other party, is intended to be the criterion by which disbursements are made. No court nor any other person or persons should substitute its or their judgment for the discretionary decision or decisions made by the Trustee.

The Trustee is granted full and complete discretion in the application of this trust for the special needs of said beneficiary, provided no part of the

APPENDICES

corpus of this trust is used to supplement or replace public assistance benefits of any governmental agency having a legal responsibility to serve persons with disabilities or impairments from which my beneficiary is receiving at the time of my death.

XI.

It is my intent and desire and I therefore encourage my Trustee to withhold payments to any party qualified as a beneficiary under the Trusts as set forth in my Last Will & Testament that would disqualify the beneficiary from receiving any form of public assistance (financial or otherwise), or might be seized by creditors or any divorced spouse of such beneficiary.

XII.

Upon my death, I nominate and appoint _____ as Guardian of the person of my child, _____, should a formal guardianship proceeding be required.

XIV.

I hereby nominate and appoint my _____, _____, as Personal Representative of this, my Last Will and Testament, and expressly confer upon such Personal Representative, full power to administer my estate without bond or security. I further confer upon my Personal Representative full power and authority to sell and convey any part or all of my estate at public or private sale without order of any court and to borrow money for the use of my estate whenever my Personal Representative shall find it necessary and proper to do so, and to secure such by lien upon any part of my estate, without any order of any court.

XV.

In the event my named Personal Representative is unable, unwilling or disqualified from so serving, I nominate and appoint _____, to serve as successor or alternate Personal Representative, with all of the rights and duties herein conferred upon my original Personal Representative.

121

XVI.

In the event my estate should involve the possibility of a Skipping Tax, I hereby state that it is my express intention that the Trusts, as set forth above, related to my grandchildren, shall have an inclusion ratio of zero (0) for federal generation skipping transfer tax purposes. Therefore, notwithstanding anything in the Trust stated above to the contrary, my Trustee shall create at the time of the funding of said Trust, a separate non-generation skipping share to qualify as a "substantially separate and independent share" as such term is defined in Treasury Regulations Sections 1.663(c)-3 and 26.2654-1, as then amended.

XVII.

I hereby direct my Trustee to use the law firm of _____, to handle all legal matters in which the Trustee requires legal assistance in the administration of this trust.

STATE OF FLORIDA
COUNTY OF _____

IN WITNESS WHEREOF, I, _____, declare to the officer taking my acknowledgment of this instrument, and to the subscribing witnesses, that I signed this instrument as my Last Will and Testament, this _____ day of _____, _____.

_____, Testator

Signed by _____, the Testator, as and for his Last Will and Testament in the presence of us, who, at his request and in his presence and in the presence of each other, have hereunto subscribed our names as witnesses the day and year first above written.

_____ at Clearwater, Florida

_____ at Clearwater, Florida

APPENDICES

We, _____, the Testator, and and _____, the witnesses, respectively, have been sworn by the officer signing below, and declare to that officer on our oaths that the Testator declared the instrument to be the Testator's will and signed it in our presence and that we each signed the instrument as a witness in the presence of the Testator and of each other and that to the best of the knowledge of each witness, the Testator was at the time eighteen (18) or more years of age, of sound mind and under no constraint or undue influence.

_____, Testator

_____
Witness

_____
Witness

Acknowledged and subscribed before me by the Testator, _____, who ( ) is personally known to me or who (   ) has produced _____as identification, and sworn to and subscribed before me by the witnesses,   , who (   ) is personally known to me or who (   ) has produced _____ as identification, and _____, who is personally known to me or who has produced   as identification, and subscribed by me in the presence of the Testator and the subscribing witnesses, all on _____ day of _____, _____.

(Seal)   _____
                          Notary Public
                          My commission expires

Courtesy of Elwood Hogan Jr., McFarland, Gould, Lyons, Sullivan & Hogan PA

APPENDIX D

CONFIDENTIAL ESTATE PLANNING QUESTIONNAIRE

YOU

Signature Name _____
(name most often used to title property and accounts)

Also Known As _____
(other names used to title property and accounts)

Prefer to be called _____

Birth Date_____

Soc. Security No._____

Employer_____

Occupation_____

Work Phone_____

E-mail address _____

U.S. Citizen?   YES   NO

State of Domicile _____

APPENDICES

YOUR SPOUSE

Signature Name _____
(name most often used to title property and accounts)

Also Known As _____
(other names used to title property and accounts)

Prefer to be called _____

Birth Date_____

Soc. Security No._____

Employer_____

Occupation_____

Work Phone_____

E-mail address _____

U.S. Citizen?   YES   NO

State of Domicile _____

Date of Marriage _____

Home Address _____

Home Phone (___)_____

City, State, Zip _____

County of Residence _____

Secondary Address _____

Secondary Phone (_____)_____

City, State, Zip _____

CHILDREN

CHILD 1

FULL NAME_____

Date of Birth _____ Occupation_____

Address (if different than yours) _____

Home Phone:_____ Business Phone: _____

Name of Spouse: _____ Occupation_____

CHILD 2

FULL NAME_____

Date of Birth _____ Occupation_____

Address (if different than yours) _____

Home Phone:_____ Business Phone: _____

Name of Spouse: _____ Occupation_____

CHILD 3

FULL NAME_____

Date of Birth _____ Occupation_____

Address (if different than yours) _____

Home Phone:_____ Business Phone: _____

Name of Spouse: _____ Occupation_____

CHILD 4

FULL NAME_____

Date of Birth _____ Occupation_____

Address (if different than yours) _____

Home Phone:_____ Business Phone: _____

Name of Spouse: _____ Occupation_____

CHILD 5

FULL NAME_____

Date of Birth _____ Occupation_____

Address (if different than yours) _____

Home Phone:_____ Business Phone: _____

Name of Spouse: _____ Occupation_____

GRANDCHILDREN

Grandchild 1

Full Name / Occupation _____ / _____

Date of Birth _____ Parents_____

Address _____ — _____

Grandchild 2

Full Name / Occupation _____ / _____

Date of Birth _____ Parents_____

Address _____

Grandchild 3

Full Name / Occupation _____ / _____

Date of Birth _____ Parents_____

Address _____

Grandchild 4

Full Name / Occupation _____ / _____

Date of Birth _____ Parents_____

Address _____

Grandchild 5

Full Name / Occupation _____/_____

Date of Birth _____ Parents_____

Address _____

Grandchild 6

Full Name / Occupation _____/_____

Date of Birth _____ Parents_____

Address _____

OTHER DEPENDENTS: Do you have anyone who depends on you for all or part of their support?

_____

_____

APPENDICES

PARENTS (YOU)

Father's Name _____ Health_____

Address_____

Age or Date of Death_____ Estimated Size of Estate _____

Mother's Name _____ Health_____

Address_____

Age or Date of Death_____ Estimated Size of Estate _____

PARENTS (YOUR SPOUSE)

Father's Name _____ Health_____

Address_____

Age or Date of Death_____ Estimated Size of Estate _____

Mother's Name _____ Health_____

Address_____

Age or Date of Death_____ Estimated Size of Estate _____

SIBLINGS (YOU)

Name: _____ Age _____ Name: _____ Age _____

Occupation _____ State ____ Occupation _____ State ___

Name: _____ Age _____ Name: _____ Age _____

Occupation _____ State ____ Occupation _____ State ___

SIBLINGS (YOUR SPOUSE)

Name: _____ Age _____ Name: _____ Age _____
Occupation _____ State ___ Occupation _____ State __

GENERAL MEDICAL CARE

Family/Attending Physician (You)

Name:_____ Phone:_____

Address:_____

Family/Attending Physician (Your Spouse)

Name:_____ Phone:_____

Address:_____

IMPORTANT QUESTIONS

Do you have any serious medical condition that we should know about?

           YES   **NO**

Have you or your spouse ever had a Will or Trust?

           YES   **NO**

Do any of your children/beneficiaries receive government support or benefits because of a disability or handicap?

           YES   **NO**

Do any of your children/beneficiaries have special educational, medical or physical needs?   **YES**   **NO**

Do you have any adopted children?

           YES   **NO**

APPENDICES

Have you or your spouse ever signed a pre or post marital agreement?

YES   **NO**

Do you or your spouse have children from a previous marriage?

YES   **NO**

Do you own or operate a family business?

YES   **NO**

Have you or your spouse ever filed a federal or state gift tax return?

YES   **NO**

Are there any charities or causes which you would like to support?

YES   **NO**

If you answered "YES" to any of these questions, please share any details which you think would be helpful.

_____

_____

PROFESSIONAL ADVISORS   **PHONE NUMBER**

Accountant _____   _____
Financial Planner _____   _____
Insurance Agent _____   _____

Financial Information
Owner: JT=Joint, H=Husband, W=Wife
Please attach copies of account statements, policies, deeds, or other asset information listed below.

Income	Amount	Source
You		
Your Spouse		

REAL ESTATE Address	Mortgage	Owner	Type	Fair Market Value
TOTAL:				$

Personal Assets	Type	Owner	Value
Personal Property	Home Furnishings		
Vehicles			
Watercrafts			
Collectibles			
Jewelry			
Other:			
TOTAL:			$

APPENDICES

Business Assets	Type	Owner	Value
TOTAL:			$

Cash Accounts Bank/Institution	Type-i.e., checking, savings, money market	Owner	Account No.	Value
TOTAL:				$

C.D.'s			
Bank/Institution	Owner	Maturity Date	Value
TOTAL:			$

U. S. Savings Bonds	Owner	Value
TOTAL:		$

Investment Accounts	Location	Owner	Cost Basis	Value
TOTAL:				$

Retirement Accounts Name/ Institution	Account No.	Type: IRA, 401K, SEP, Keogh, etc.	Owner	Beneficiary	Value
TOTAL:					$

APPENDICES

Stock Options Company	Type: NQ or ISO	Owner	Vesting Date	Current Value
TOTAL:				$

Life Insurance	Owner	Premium	Cash Value	Insured	Beneficiary	Death Benefit
TOTAL:						$

Children's Accounts	Owner	Value
TOTAL:		$

Other – Description	Owner	Value
TOTAL:		$

INSIDE THE MINDS

Liabilities - Owed to:	Comments	Value
TOTAL:		$

NET WORTH	
Total Assets (excluding life insurance)	$
Total Liabilities	$
Net Worth (excluding life insurance)	$
Total Retirement Assets (included above)	$
Total Life Insurance	$

Courtesy of Brad A. Galbraith, Hahn Loeser & Parks LLP

APPENDIX E

OBJECTIVES WORKSHEET

1. I want to create a consistent and comprehensive estate plan which includes my own health care plan.

2. I want to plan for my elderly parents.

3. I want to preserve my privacy.

4. I want to reduce estate and death taxes to the lowest possible level.

5. I want to avoid probate and minimize settlement expenses for my family.

6. I want to plan for disability of me or my spouse and avoid court conservatorship.

7. I want to avoid unnecessary placement in a nursing home by planning for in-home health care.

8. I want to protect my children from a failed marriage by preventing their divorced spouse from taking my child's inheritance.

9. I want to protect my assets from unforeseen future lawsuits and claims against me.

10. I want to disinherit one or more of my children or other family members.

11. I want to plan for my grandchildren directly rather than have them receive their parent's share of my estate.

12. I want to plan the transfer and survival of the family business.

13. I have one or more pets that should be protected and cared for.

14. I want to control all of my own assets while I am alive and healthy.

15. I want to save 100% of the estate tax on my life insurance so that all proceeds can pass to my heirs estate tax free.

16. I want to create a special tax exempt trust to which I can transfer some of my assets for a lifetime income and to avoid capital gains tax.

17. I want to control who will make health care decisions for me in the event of my incapacity.

18. I want to protect my children's inheritance in the event my surviving spouse chooses to remarry after my death.

19. I want to plan for a child with disabilities or special needs.

20. I want to plan for my children from a previous marriage.

21. I want to leave an endowment for my church or favorite charities.

22. I want to update my closely-held company's organizational book and records so that it is in compliance with state and federal requirements.

Courtesy of Brad A. Galbraith, Hahn Loeser & Parks LLP

APPENDICES

APPENDIX F

LEGACY MANAGEMENT PROGRAM

The literary components of any great story come down to the essentials of who, what, when, where and why. These questions are used to build continuity and themes to the teller's work. In the same fashion, when one looks to define a legacy, these same basic components are used to measure experiences and form life stories.

At Hahn Loeser, we have mastered the art of legacy planning and recognize each life story is unique and constantly affected by change. That is why we have created our Legacy Management Program. This systemized updating program provides ongoing support and continued education for our firm's legacy planning clients. The Legacy Management Program provides the necessary services to assure plans stay current by offering the following:

- Year 1 Strategic Funding. Review status of legacy plan strategic funding.
- Year 2 Custom Instructions. Review and update custom personal instructions.
- Year 3 Legacy Plan Review. In-person conference to review and revise your plan for any changes in the law or in your objectives.
- Ongoing Support. Continued funding assistance. Personal amendments.
- Continued Education. Monthly firm newsletters. Successor trustee training workshops.

At Hahn Loeser we are committed to our clients' life story. We recognize that updating legacy plans is essential for individuals and families' financial strength. For more information on our Legacy Management Program, contact Brad A. Galbraith at 317.578.1400 (Indianapolis, Indiana) or 239.593.0996 (Naples, Florida).

Courtesy of Brad A. Galbraith, Hahn Loeser & Parks LLP